Renewing Your Mind
40 Devotional

40 Days of Reflection, Refreshing and Revival

By
J.C. MATTHEWS

BLESSED BOOKS
PUBLISHING CO.

J.C. MATTHEWS

Published by Blessed Books Publishing Co.
P.O. Box 360102
Irving, TX 75063

J.C. MATTHEWS

Table of Contents

J.C. MATTHEWS

J.C. MATTHEWS

J.C. MATTHEWS

"And do not be conformed to this world, but be transformed by the renewing of your mind, that you may prove what is that good and acceptable and perfect will of God."
Romans 12:2

J.C. MATTHEWS

1

Divine Direction

*"Then some Midianite traders passed by, so they
pulled him up and lifted Joseph out of the pit,
and sold him to the Ishmaelites for twenty
shekels of silver. Thus they brought Joseph into
Egypt."*
Genesis 3:28

Often, when we look for direction from God we seek the
miraculous. We search for a sign, a voice or a vision to
make our paths plain. However, God can and does employ
more common (even painful) experiences in our lives to provide
direction in our lives. We lose a job, experience a break up in a
relationship, financial instability, stricken with an illness or
something is taken from us. Often these tools of direction are

J.C. MATTHEWS

employed when He has tried to get our attention to turn in another direction by speaking to us, but His words were not heeded. These "life events" may be God's way of causing us to look in another direction. God will often close a door, to point us in the direction of another.

God has a purpose and plan for our lives. The problem is – *so do we.* Often our plans and God's plan are not the same. In making our plans, we often seek short sighted objectives and solutions to our problems. God knows this and allows certain events in our lives to point us in the right direction that leads to our destinies. Often the situations that God's directions lead us into look nothing like what we think God's plan for our lives should look like. We must be careful not to misconstrue God's *direction* as *persecution. "God causes all things to work together for good to those who love God, to those who are called according to His purpose"* (Romans 8:28).

If anyone's life demonstrates this principle it's that of Joseph found in the book of Genesis. As a child, Joseph received a dream from God revealing his destiny. In his dream he was in a place of prestige and power. In a short period of time, Joseph went from being his father's favorite son to being a slave in a foreign land. He was thrown into a pit, sold into slavery and taken to Egypt to spend the rest of his life.

Unbeknownst to Joseph, all of this was God's way of positioning him to fulfill his purpose in life. It was "divine direction". Joseph had to go into the pit, to meet Potiphar. Potiphar's wife had to falsely accuse Joseph of rape for him to receive a life sentence in federal prison. It was in prison where Joseph had the opportunity to met a couple of attendants in Pharaoh's court. Because Joseph carried himself with integrity, even in this seemingly hopeless situation, did he receive the opportunity to meet Pharaoh himself. When he met Pharaoh he was finally promoted to the place of destiny that God showed him when he was back in his father's house. It was all divine direction!

When Joseph laid his head down to sleep that first night in Egypt he was far from home, but squarely within God's plan. When his brother betrayed him and threw him in the pit, he never thought that he just took the first step in fulfilling his destiny. His situation looked nothing like his destination, because God does things differently than men do them. God declares: *For My thoughts are not your thoughts, Nor are your ways My ways," declares the LORD. "For as the heavens are higher than the earth, So are My ways higher than your ways And My thoughts than your thoughts (Isaiah 55:8-9).*

J.C. MATTHEWS

I am sure Joseph saw the changes in his situation as set backs, when in reality they were setups. God was providing *"divine direction"* through what appeared to be certain disaster. Each disappointing turn in his life took him one step closer to realizing his destiny and purpose.

Some of you may be experiencing what appears to be disaster or you may have come to what appears to be a dead end in your life, when in fact it's direction. As you experience your transition, never lose sight of God's sovereignty. Sometimes God allows us to lose control so that He can take control. When Joseph's brothers threw him into the pit, I am sure he had no idea he had taken the first step toward his destiny. After looking over his life and all that had transpired, Joseph was able to say to the ones who tried to kill him:

> *"As for you, you meant evil against me, but God meant it for good in order to bring about this present result"* (Genesis 50:20).

Everything he thought was an accident was really divine providence. It was God providing *divine direction!*

J.C. MATTHEWS

Personal Meditations

What is God saying to me through this word?

_____

_____

_____

What adjustments or steps must I take to apply this word in
my life?

_____

_____

_____

How has this word affected my approach to, and outlook upon,
my life?

_____

_____

_____

Personal Notes & Thoughts:

_____

_____

_____

J.C. MATTHEWS

J.C. MATTHEWS

2

Shake It Off!

*"Whoever does not receive you, nor heed your
words, as you go out of that house or that city,
shake the dust off your feet."*
Matthew 10:14

As Jesus began to prepare His disciples for their calling as leaders in the Church, He decided they needed to go out on their own and learn to do what they had previously seen Him do. For soon Jesus would no longer be physically with them and they needed to know who to operate in His absence. So He gathered the disciples together and instructed them to go out into the surrounding cities to preach and demonstrate the Kingdom of God. At the very end of His instructions, Jesus

J.C. MATTHEWS

tells his disciples to do something, that is not as spectacular as His other instructions, but is essential to their having success in what they have been assigned to do. This essential piece of wisdom that Jesus shared with his disciples has just as much application and revelation for us today, as it did when He originally spoke these words over 2000 years ago.

Jesus first instructs His disciples to take no money for their journey, preach the Kingdom of Heaven, heal the sick, raise the dead, cleanse the lepers, cast out demons and when it is all said and done - know when to "shake the dust off".

Jesus said that their ability to shake off criticism, rejection, opposition and other people's opinion of them was just as important as their preaching the gospel, healing the sick, raising the dead, cleansing lepers and casting out demons. Jesus knew that their ability to overcome persecution and rejection was critical to their ability to succeed at what He told them to do. If they succumbed to criticism and rejection, there would be no preaching, healing, raising or cleansing because they would quit and abandon what they were sent to do.

We too must learn to shake off the dust that others cast upon us to stop us and move forward in life. There are times in life when we will have to go at it alone! If you never learn to shake off what life and others will place upon you, you will find

14

yourself bound and unable to move forward in life because you're carrying things and burdens that God never intended for you to carry.

Not only must we learn to shake off the dirt that others place upon us, but we must also learn to shake off the dirt that we've accumulated and held onto over the years. There are things in our pasts that have clung to us to remind us of what we used to be. This dirt may be failures, words that have wounded us or mistakes we've made that we are trying to make up for that hinder us in moving forward into our assignments and callings. Many of the disciples had less than desirable pasts that they had to shake off and move forward despite their history. There was Matthew the tax collector who had to shake of the guilt, shame and condemnation of his past occupation in order to move forward in the ministry that Christ had given him. If Matthew had not learned to shake off what he knew about himself, and what others were saying about him, he would not have been able to minister with the conviction and power necessary for him to do what Christ instructed him to do. The enemy will use other people's attitudes and opinions to try to cause you to doubt yourself and forfeit what God has for you.

What is it that you've allowed to lay dormant because of rejection, opposition or someone's opinion of you? Has someone

J.C. MATTHEWS

said something to you that has caused you to doubt yourself, your ability, purpose or future? If so, do what Jesus told His disciples to do – *"shake it off"* and keep moving!

J.C. MATTHEWS

Personal Meditations

What is God saying to me through this word?

_____

_____

_____

What adjustments or steps must I take to apply this word in
my life?

_____

_____

_____

How has this word affected my approach to, and outlook upon,
my life?

_____

_____

_____

Personal Notes & Thoughts:

_____

_____

_____

J.C. MATTHEWS

J.C. MATTHEWS

3

Hearing and Knowing God's Voice

"Abraham stretched out his hand and took the knife to slay his son. But the angel of the LORD called to him from heaven and said, "Abraham, Abraham!" And he said, "Here I am." He said, "Do not stretch out your hand against the lad, and do nothing to him" (Genesis 22:10-12, NASB).

I can remember driving from Cincinnati, Ohio to Dallas, Texas for the first time. We had never made this trip before so I took a road map with us. Everything was going as planned until we encountered road construction. In trying to follow the detour signage, I took a wrong turn and we became lost. Fortunately, I had the satellite based OnStar system. I pressed a button and a voice came through the sound system pinpointing my present location and gave me turn-by-turn directions through the unfamiliar territory. I found my way back to the highway and eventually to Dallas by listening to a voice and following the same map I started my journey with. There was never anything wrong with the map and at no time did the voice contradict what the map said. However, the map was printed before the road construction began. The directions OnStar gave me were also based upon a map, but specifically took into consideration my present situation.

Likewise, it is necessary for Believers today, to not only know God's Word, but also be able to *hear* and *discern* His voice. In the above situation, the map represented the Bible and OnStar represented the voice of God. Both were necessary for me to reach my intended destination. Both were accurate and never contradicted the other. Having access to both, allowed me to avoid danger and my suffering loss.

It is inevitable that we will encounter situations in life that throw us off course, causing us to find ourselves in places and situations we never intended on being. God may even lead us to places where we can't find our own way out for the purpose of teaching us to discern and hear His voice. There are some levels of blessing and ministry that we will never be able to enjoy until we are able to hear God's voice. It is our ability to

J.C. MATTHEWS

recognize His voice that distinguishes us as belonging to Him. Jesus said, *"My sheep hear My voice, and I know them, and they follow Me"* (John 10:27).

It is even possible to know God's Word and not His voice. Seminary can teach you His Word, but it can't teach you to hear His voice. This ability is developed through your familiarity and intimacy with God. Like a mother who can distinguish her child's cry in the midst of a room of crying children, we must grow to the point in our relationship with God where we can distinguish His voice above all the others.

The importance of not only knowing "*what God has said* "but also "*what God is saying*" is demonstrated in the life of Abraham. Abraham clearly heard God's instruction to sacrifice his son Isaac. That is what God *said* to him. When Abraham reached the place where Isaac was to be sacrificed, he heard God's voice again *saying*, *"Do nothing to him"*. This is what God *was saying*. Same God. Same voice. Different purpose. Abraham's ability to hear and discern God's voice in the midst of his situation saved Isaac's life. If Abraham had not grown to know and heed God's voice he would have killed the very thing God sent to be a blessing in his life.

God does not always speak audibly, but He is always speaking. He speaks through our relationships, finances, losses and

J.C. MATTHEWS

victories. He speaks through doors that are open and those that are closed. God's voice provides us the needed direction for the various situations that arise in life.

Do you know God's voice? If God were to speak to you today would you be able to discern His voice above all others? Are you feeling lost or confused about what to do next or whether you are presently doing what is best? If so, set aside some time alone with Him. Listen closely, you may discover that God has already provided the direction you've been seeking – you just couldn't discern His voice.

Personal Meditations

What is God saying to me through this word?

_____

_____

_____

What adjustments or steps must I take to apply this word in
my life?

_____

_____

_____

How has this word affected my approach to, and outlook upon,
my life?

_____

_____

_____

Personal Notes & Thoughts:

_____

_____

_____

J.C. MATTHEWS

J.C. MATTHEWS

4

Believe It to See It

"I had fainted, unless I had believed to see the goodness of the LORD in the land of the living. Wait on the LORD: be of good courage, and he shall strengthen thine heart: wait, I say, on the LORD" (Psalms 27:13-14, KJV).

Many of us over the years were taught that, *"seeing is believing"*. As a result of this, our situations look much like those around us because it is all we've learned to believe God for. David understood that one of the most important decisions he could make in his life was to be selective in *what he chose to believe.*

J.C. MATTHEWS

As a matter of fact, it was what he believed that kept him from fainting when he faced seemingly hopeless and impossible situations. If you were to read the entire 27th Psalms you would find that David faced some pretty stressful and seemingly hopeless situations. In this Psalm, he was surrounded by enemies who were committed to utterly destroying him. However, in the face of all of this, David was able to maintain his composure and gain the victory by holding onto what he believed. Lets take a look at what David believed so that we too may learn the secret to overcoming the things that we must face.

First, *"You must believe that you will see what you've been asking God for"*.

No matter how dark and grim the situation may appear you must maintain an expectation that better will come. Better yet, expect that better is on its way. Your ability to see what it is that you're believing God for, allows you to *receive it* before you *see it*. As a matter of fact this is necessary. The text says that David would have fainted *"unless"* he had "*believed to see*" what it was he hoped for. His belief that he would *see* something better enabled him to stand instead of fainting while he was waiting.

J.C. MATTHEWS

Second, *"You must know that God's goodness is greater than your situation"*

David's focus was on his problem, but on *"the goodness of the Lord".* He proclaimed in Psalms 23, *"surely goodness and mercy will follow me all the days of my life"*. He was being hunted by his enemies, while at the same time being shadowed by God's goodness. He didn't say *maybe*– but *"surely goodness ... will follow me"*! Do you believe this? Even in the midst of your situation? God's goodness may not keep you from trouble but it will keep you through the trouble. Your trouble is an opportunity for you to become acquainted with God's goodness (Ps. 27:5). I never knew how good God was until I learned to lean on His goodness.

Finally, *"You must believe that God wants to bless you <u>now</u> – in this life".*

God wants to bless you now – while you are still alive – here on earth - today! Too many Believers' expectation of being blessed is only in the after life in heaven, when they live their life enduring situations that they should be overcoming. Make no mistake, Heaven is going to be grand, but God has given you a life to live here on earth, which includes experiencing His goodness. Life is not all about suffering, pain, loss and grief. *"Life is your license to experience God's goodness in the land of the living."* That is the here and now!

It is my suspicion that many of you are facing situations that cause you to feel as if you are about to faint. The problem may be that you don't believe that you will ever see anything better. You must develop a conviction that it is God's will that you experience His goodness in this life. God has not brought you this far for you to fail. If failure was your outcome, He did not have to bring you through the last battle that threatened to end it all. His plan is that you win. He has some goodness for you in this life. However, you must believe it, in order for you to see it!

Personal Meditations

What is God saying to me through this word?

_____

_____

_____

What adjustments or steps must I take to apply this word in
my life?

_____

_____

_____

How has this word affected my approach to, and outlook upon,
my life?

_____

_____

_____

Personal Notes & Thoughts:

_____

_____

_____

J.C. MATTHEWS

J.C. MATTHEWS

5

"Tell It!"

"And they overcame him by the blood of the Lamb, and by the word of their testimony; and they loved not their lives unto the death."
Revelations 12:11, KJV

I discovered something while a student in law school that shed light on why so many people are bound by situations they should be set free from. During an Evidence class, we came to the topic of "Testimony". In summary, I discovered that testimony serves the purpose of proving the truthfulness of a matter by the confirmation of another who has (preferably) first hand knowledge of the events. This person is called a *"witness"*. This individual only qualifies as a witness if they have *"first hand knowledge or experience"* of the matter. The most powerful testimony a witness can possess is *"eye witness" testimony.* The testimony offered by a witness who lacks this first hand knowledge is categorized as *"hearsay".* Hearsay has very little probative value and is often excluded from being accepted into evidence. Oftentimes, the freedom, and very life, of the one being tried depends on eyewitnesses that are *willing to testify* concerning what they know.

As I read Revelations 12:11, it occurred to me that many people are unnecessarily bound and perishing in their trials because the enemy has shamed witnesses from coming forward and testifying about their our own experiences and what they know. The enemy knows that our testimony has the power to defeat him and set the accused free. Many people are serving life sentences in bondage, condemnation, and some even losing their lives, because they've lost all hope of things getting better or them surviving what they're going through. However, we are living testimonies or evidence that they *can in fact* make it. The enemy tried to destroy our bodies, minds/souls and spirits – but failed. Our testimony proves that the devil is a liar and defeated!

Testimony, by its very nature, is not for the one testifying but for the benefit of the one being tried. I don't care how shameful your past may have been; someone else needs the

32

deliverance that is in *your mouth*. There is a ministry in your testimony that cannot be denied or refuted. Proverbs 18:21 declares, that the *"power of life and death is in the tongue"*.

It is interesting to note that the root word for *"testimony"* in the Greek is *"martus"*. It is the same word from which we get the word "martyr". A martyr is someone who died for what they believe and know to be true. I mentioned earlier, that "hearsay" testimony is generally not accepted as evidence. However, there are exceptions to this rule. One such exception concerns the *"words of a dying or dead person"*. These words are considered unusually reliable because a dying or dead person (1) has not ongoing interest in the matter, and (2) has nothing to lose by telling the truth. They are no longer subject to fear, intimidation or the power of those who have an interest in the outcome of a matter. They're free to tell the truth, the whole truth and nothing but the truth, so help them God!

As born again, blood washed, forgiven Believers, who are dead to all the guilt and shame of our past, why aren't we testifying to what we've experienced and been delivered from? It is all under the blood, buried in the watery grave of baptism and crucified with our old man. Our past has no power over us! We are free to tell it – all of it! There is no more condemnation to those who are in Christ Jesus (Romans 8:1). When and if we fall short, we can pray for forgiveness and God forgives us, never to be brought to our charge again.

With this being the case, let me ask you a question: *What are you afraid of? What's keeping you from testifying to others of what God has brought you out of and delivered you from?* Others are struggling with the same thing you've been delivered from and need to know the truth – *that God is a deliverer!*

The text says, *"they overcame him by the blood of the Lamb, and by the word of their testimony."* Jesus has done His part in defeating the enemy. He shed His blood and rose from the grave. Now we must do our part by *telling our testimony!* Every time you *"tell it"*, it reminds the devil he is *"defeated!"* Go ahead - remember what He's done for you! Don't be afraid or ashamed - just *"tell it!"*

J.C. MATTHEWS

Personal Meditations

What is God saying to me through this word?

_____

_____

_____

What adjustments or steps must I take to apply this word in
my life?

_____

_____

_____

How has this word affected my approach to, and outlook upon,
my life?

_____

_____

_____

Personal Notes & Thoughts:

_____

_____

_____

J.C. MATTHEWS

J.C. MATTHEWS

6

Get Up and Wash Your Face!

"David therefore pleaded with God for the child, and David fasted and went in and lay all night on the ground. .David perceived that the child was dead. Therefore David said to his servants, "Is the child dead?" And they said, "He is dead." So David arose from the ground, washed and anointed himself, and changed his clothes; and he went into the house of the Lord and worshiped." (2 Samuel 12:18, NKJ).

Life doesn't stop just because we've been hurt, lost something or dealing with a difficult situation. It doesn't slow down because we are tired or need help – it keeps on moving. Before you know it, something else is coming your way and if you don't get moving – it too will run you over. Therefore, we must learn how to properly respond too and effectively deal with the varying transitions and seasons in our lives.

David had a son born out of an adulterous relationship with Bathsheba. Because of David's sin, God declared that the child would die. During this turbulent time, David refused any comforts offered him and laid prostrate before the Lord in heaviness. However, the day came when he realized his worst fear– *his son died.* David's response to this news shocked those around him but demonstrates a principle that we too must apply when dealing with hardship in our lives. The Bible says that upon receiving the news that his son was dead, David: (1) *Got up*, (2) *washed and anointed himself,* (3) *changed his clothes*, and (4) went to church and *worshipped.* Many of you may be saying, *"Wait a minute!" "His son just died!?"* Yes, this is true. But David realized that there was nothing he could do about it. So, David got up and started to deal with the things that were still within his control. David decided to *live the rest of his life*. It was his son that died, not him.

David told me to tell you: **First,** you need to *"get up"* from where you fell. Don't become stuck at the place of your loss. I call these places *"gravesites"*. Gravesite are places you visit to *remember* a loss. They were never intended to be the *residence* for the living. Gravesites are places you *stop by* – but don't

38

stay. **Secondly**, you must *wash* and *anoint yourself.* David knew that whatever it was that *he did*, it did not determine *who he was.* He was God's anointed. You may have made some mistakes in your life, but they do not define "who" you are. You must learn to wash your past off and walk in the anointing that God has declared over your life. **Thirdly**, *change your clothes.* You should not look like where you came from but where you are headed. These clothes may be old associations, habits or thoughts that are remnants of your past. Take them off and put on that which communicates your future, not your past! **Last, but not least**, *worship God!* The reason we become stuck in *weeping* is because we neglect to *worship.* In loss or gain, sickness or health, ups or downs – God is still worthy of your worship. When we understand that regardless of our situation, God is still God; we allow Him to do what only God can do in our lives.

Maybe there is something in your life that you wish you could change - but can't. You've been trying to make amends for something that you can do nothing about. The Bible says that after David's son died that He worshipped, took Bathsheba as his wife, and God replaced what He had taken – another son named Solomon. Restoration will not happen until you decide to *"get up and wash your face!"*

J.C. MATTHEWS

Personal Meditations

What is God saying to me through this word?

_____

_____

_____

What adjustments or steps must I take to apply this word in my life?

_____

_____

_____

How has this word affected my approach to, and outlook upon, my life?

_____

_____

_____

Personal Notes & Thoughts:

_____

_____

_____

J.C. MATTHEWS

7

"Bring It To Me"

"A man came up to Jesus, falling on his knees before Him and saying, 'Lord, have mercy on my son, for he is a lunatic and is very ill; ... I brought him to Your disciples, and they could not cure him. ' And Jesus answered and said ... 'Bring him here to Me."
Matthew 17:14-17, NASB

In life there are problems that I call "God problems." These are not problems with God, but problems only God can handle. God problems are those that cannot be fixed with your checkbook, education or influence. These problems are outside of the control of human beings and lie squarely within God's sovereign jurisdiction. They stop us in our tracks and cause us to soberly assess our associations and situations in life. They bring us face to face with our insufficiency and our need for

J.C. MATTHEWS

God's sufficiency. When we face a God problem we discover what is really important in life. These problems are not designed to stop us from making progress in life, but to reveal our dependency on God for everything in life. God wants to reveal something to you and your problem may be the vehicle He is using to do it.

Throughout the gospels people sought Jesus to do what no one else could do. In Matthew 17:14-17, a father had a son who was demon-possessed and no one else was able to help him, including Jesus' disciples. Finally, the father encounters Jesus. Jesus, looking at this seemingly impossible and long term situation, tells the father to, *"Bring him to Me"*. Jesus did in a moment what others could not do!

In another situation, the disciples faced a seemingly impossible task of feeding over 5000 men (not including the women and children) with two fish and five loaves of bread. After taking inventory of the situation, Jesus, speaking of the fish and loaves, tells the disciples to, "Bring them here to me." Having placed their impossible situation in the hands of Jesus, the peoples' insufficiency was transformed into over flowing sufficiency. So much so, that there were 12 baskets full of leftovers after everyone had eaten their fill.

42

J.C. MATTHEWS

Too often, God is the last stop in our search for help. We don't have to lose everything before we begin to seek Him. God is not intimidated by what we are dealing with. We must stop trying to fix our problem on our own and seek God for our deliverance.

Let's be honest, if we could fix it, it would have been fixed by now. This is a "God Problem", or a "problem *for* God". Don't mistake your trusting people with trusting God. When God showed up, deliverance quickly followed.

I want to challenge you. Set aside some time in the morning, evening, on your lunch break or when you are lying in bed, and seek out God's presence. Block out your situation and focus on God's promises. In Matthew 11:28-30, Jesus promised, *"Come to Me, all who are weary and heavy-laden, and I will give you rest. Take My yoke upon you and learn from Me, ... 'For My yoke is easy and My burden is light'."*

This offer still stands for those who will seek Him! No matter how long you've had the problem. NO matter how big it is. Whatever it is, God still says to - *"bring it to Me!"*

J.C. MATTHEWS

Personal Meditations

What is God saying to me through this word?

_____

_____

_____

What adjustments or steps must I take to apply this word in
my life?

_____

_____

_____

How has this word affected my approach to, and outlook upon,
my life?

_____

_____

_____

Personal Notes & Thoughts:

_____

_____

_____

J.C. MATTHEWS

8

Facilitating the Flow

Then he said, "Go, borrow vessels at large for yourself from all your neighbors, {even} empty vessels; do not get a few. "...."So she went from him and shut the door behind her and her sons; they were bringing {the vessels} to her and she poured. When the vessels were full, she said to her son, "Bring me another vessel." And he said to her, "There is not one vessel more." And the oil stopped" (2 Kings 4:3-6, NASB).

Every time I read this passage of scripture, I can't help but wonder what the possibilities could have been if the widow would have recognized the opportunity God had laid before her. God released a flow in her life whose only limitation was the one she placed upon it.

This woman was the widow of a man who served God and died with unpaid debts. As a result, a creditor was coming to take her sons as slaves in payment of the debt. She approached the man of God expecting that he would give her something to change her situation. However, the man of God causes her to look at her situation from another perspective. He basically said to her, your deliverance is not in what I or anyone else can give you, but in what you already possess. He asked her: *"What do you have in the house?"* In essence, he said to her: You already possess enough to handle your situation. Upon further inspection of her situation she replies, *"Your maidservant has <u>nothing in the house</u> **except** a jar of oil."* What she considered to be *"nothing"*, was the very same thing God used to not only deliver her from debt, but gave her and her sons the opportunity to live debt free for the rest of their lives.

The man of God gave her an action plan that involved her using the little she had combined with her faith in God's Word. He instructs her to borrow as many vessels as she could and to pour the little oil she has into them. She obeys this seemingly irrational request and somehow, some way, they are filled with oil. Then, something *tragic* happens. The Bible says, *"the oil stopped."* Did God run out of oil, power or provision? Never! Then what happened? Why did the oil stop? *The oil stopped*
46

because she had no more capacity to handle the flow God initiated in her life.

As I thought about the widow's situation, God revealed to me that the same thing is happening in the lives of Believers around the world. They pray to God to meet their needs, but have not developed the capacity to receive what they've asked for. Their lack of preparation for His provision limits God in what He can do for them. This woman could have seized the opportunity and went into the *oil business!* With vision to see beyond her present circumstance and a plan for the future, she could have sent her sons to the market, not only sell the oil they'd received, but to buy larger pots (barrels even) with the profits made from the sale of the oil. As long as there was a prepared place - God was committed to fill it. Once there was no place found, God stopped the flow, rather than commit waste. Remember, with every provision of God comes limitless opportunity.

What do you have in your possession that God could use to create a flow in your life? It could be something tangible, intangible or what I call an "in house"; like a special ability, skill or vision God has given you. Whatever He gave *to you,* He intends for it to provide *for you.* You may already have in your midst the answer to your prayers. However, there may not be

J.C. MATTHEWS

enough room for God to manifest what He wants to do in your life! Are you prepared? If not, get ready and prepare a place to facilitate the flow that God wants to send your way!

Personal Meditations

What is God saying to me through this word?

_____

_____

_____

What adjustments or steps must I take to apply this word in my life?

_____

_____

_____

How has this word affected my approach to, and outlook upon, my life?

_____

_____

_____

Personal Notes & Thoughts:

_____

_____

_____

J.C. MATTHEWS

J.C. MATTHEWS

9

Rearview Mirrors

"Brethren, I count not myself to have apprehended: but this one thing I do, forgetting those things which are behind, and reaching forth unto those things which are before, I press toward the mark for the prize of the high calling of God in Christ Jesus" (Philippians 3:13-14, KJV).

*Some of the greatest obstacles in life are not the things that lie in our **"paths"** but those things that are in our **"pasts"**.*

A proper perspective and appreciation for our past will allow us to glean the wisdom gained from our experiences, while at the same time prevent us from becoming hostage to them.

I've heard it said that; *"The best thing one can do is to forget their past and move on into their future."* I don't exactly agree with this statement. God brought you through what you've

J.C. MATTHEWS

been through so that you *would* remember from whence you've come. Those who forget their past are bound to repeat it. Your ability to remember (not repeat) your past is a powerful weapon in the arsenal of a Believer. What you are able to remember is the *substance of your testimony*. The Bible says: *"they overcame him (the devil) because of the blood of the Lamb and because of the <u>word of their testimony</u>..."* (Revelations 12:11, underline added). Some of you may be asking: "How do I remember my past without repeating it?". My answer is: You must learn to use what I call *"rearview mirrors"*.

If you've ever driven a car you have no doubt used *rearview mirrors*. Rearview mirrors are those devices that allow you to reflect on what is behind you while enabling you to continue to face and head in the direction of your destination. We must learn to do the same thing in our lives. We must be able to reference our past while not having to turn around and lose focus of where we are going.

Whether you know it or not, God has equipped you with *rearview mirrors*. When we submit ourselves to God's Word and Will, we are in His hands. We can reflect on what we've been through while being kept secure by His Spirit. His Spirit guides and keeps us, allowing us to stand in the places that we

52

previously fell. The Word of God is a mirror that allows us to keep our past, present and future in its proper perspective. Without the mirror of God's Word and its truth, we could become condemned by our past, and rob God of the glory that is born from our testimony.

There are many people who experienced what you've experienced in your past, but did not make it out of what you experience to have a testimony. Your testimony is precious to God and powerful to those who will hear it. God has a purpose and plan for you - which also includes your past. Your past does not have to be a hindrance to your future. You must learn how to appreciate and reflect on your past, while you continue pressing into your future!

J.C. MATTHEWS

What is God saying to me through this word?

_____

_____

_____

What adjustments or steps must I take to apply this word in my life?

_____

_____

_____

How has this word affected my approach to, and outlook upon, my life?

_____

_____

_____

Personal Notes & Thoughts:

_____

_____

_____

J.C. MATTHEWS

10

It Is Well

*"When the man of God saw her at a distance, he said to
Gehazi his servant, "Behold, there is the Shunammite.
"Please run now to meet her and say to her, 'Is it well
with you? Is it well with your husband? Is it well with
the child?' " And she answered, "It is well." '*
2 Kings 4:25-26, NASB

D o you have *"It is well faith?"* *"It is well faith"* is faith
that is wholly based on the *Promisor's promise* and not
on how things appear. Can you look at your present condition
and still say, *"It is well?"* If not, you are more than likely
focusing on the wrong thing.

As sure as each moment of life brings you a moment closer toward death, you will be faced with a *factual situation* that contradicts what you are believing God for. As a matter of fact, that is what your situation is after - *your faith*. The bible says in James 1: 2-3, *"count it all joy when you fall into various trials, knowing that the testing of your faith produces patience."* The various trials were directed at their faith. Our faith is what causes us to overcome what we do see, to receive what God has said we will see, but has not manifested yet.

The enemy wants to use the *facts of our situation* to frustrate our *faith* and what God has said concerning us. Our breakthrough will be determined by our decision to stand on our **faith** and not on the **facts**. Facts change, but the Word of God never changes. Facts are based on circumstances, while faith is based on the surety of God's Word. The Bible says, *"God is not a man, that He should lie, Nor a son of man, that He should repent; Has He said, and will He not do it? Or has He spoken, and will He not make it good?"* (Numbers 23:19). The most valuable possession you can have is genuine and unshakable faith in God's Word. It is what enables you to endure and overcome hostile and oppressive living conditions. With faith, no person, thing or situation has the final word. This is why the Bible says, *"we walk (live) by faith and not by sight"* (2 Corinthians 5:7) (brackets added).

56

In the text, this Shunammite woman was materially prosperous but had no child. Because she cared for the man of God he promised her a child. She eventually had the child who grew to adulthood but later died while in the field. The woman placed her dead son on the bed of the one who promised her a son and set out to find him. When questioned about where she was going she replied, *"It will be well"*. As she approached, the prophet's servant asked how things were going and she again replied, *"It is well"*.

Her son is dead, her husband had given up on his son and when she finally finds the one who promised her a son, she doesn't cuss, faint or fight. She reminds him of God's Word. She was holding onto her faith in the Word instead of the fact that her son was dead.

Too many of us give up on things too easily because their realization seems unlikely or impossible. We have allowed blessings, callings, dreams and breakthroughs that God has sent us to die because it appeared that they would never happen. The next time you think of abandoning a dream or promise that God gave you – remember the Shunammite woman's response to facts. When the facts say *it won't work, it will never happen* or *things will never change*, say what the Shunammite woman said: *"It Is Well!"*

J.C. MATTHEWS

Personal Meditations

What is God saying to me through this word?

_____

_____

_____

What adjustments or steps must I take to apply this word in my life?

_____

_____

_____

How has this word affected my approach to, and outlook upon, my life?

_____

_____

_____

Personal Notes & Thoughts:

_____

_____

_____

J.C. MATTHEWS

11

Recognizing The Enemy

"Lest Satan should get an advantage of us: for we are not ignorant of his devices."
2 Corinthians 2:11, KJV

The key to experiencing victory in your life may lie in your ability to recognize your enemy. Can you recognize the work of the enemy in your life? Most people would say, "Yes!" However, I am convinced that a vast majority of Believers cannot? When I think of the battle that we, as Believers, must wage in life against evil, my thoughts gravitate towards the war in Iraq. Militarily, the U.S is far more powerful and sophisticated in training and weaponry, but yet and still, we are experiencing an ever-increasing number of casualties. There is a reason for this. The reason is *our enemy is hard to recognize*. The enemy in this battle does not always wear a uniform by which he can be easily identified. In many instances, it is not a *he* but a *she*. Women, children and unassuming old men are sacrificing themselves in order to inflict as much damage on the U.S. Armed forces as possible. Armed Service men and women face daily, the possibility that the person who just walked by or is eating at a diner across the street, is actually there to steal, kill and destroy any future or hope they have.

On a daily basis you and I wage war against an enemy that we cannot see and who does not want to be recognized. When most people think of evil, or picture the enemy, they visualize a man in a red suit with horns and a pitchfork. Many look for what Hollywood has depicted as evil – some wild and out of control person. Evil is much too clever to be so obvious. Satan experiences the most success in secret; carrying out covert operations in the lives of Believers. Strategically killing, stealing and destroying people's hopes, dreams and lives while going undetected. This is his primary mode of operation.

This is why Paul instructs the Corinthian church (and us) not to be ignorant of, the devices of the enemy. Many people wonder, *"How did I get in the condition that I'm in?" "How could I have done what I did?" "Why do I feel this way?" "How can I think about or meditate on such things?"* If you've thought or said any of the above, you've been attacked - and didn't know it.

You must understand that evil will very seldom come at you as full-blown evil. It will present itself as something harmless, inconsequential, small and even cloaked as something good. It does this because it knows that *"good people"* will not readily embrace something that is obviously evil, so it must appear to be something other than what it really is. This is why so many "good people" become victims to bad habits, bad relationships and find themselves in bad situations. They've allowed something that appeared good into their lives, which turned out to be something other than good.

This takes spiritual discernment. Jesus understood this and was able to discern between what appeared to be genuine concern for His well-being and demonic activity. When Jesus told His disciples of His pending suffering, Peter pulled Him aside and proclaimed that he would never let Jesus suffer. Jesus looked Peter straight in the eye and said: *"Get behind Me, Satan!"* (Matthew 16:23). What appeared to be genuine concern by a friend was actually a device of the devil. As a matter of fact, the first place we find a demon mentioned in the New Testament is in a place that we would least expect it. It was not in a graveyard, nor some dark enchanted forest - but *in church!* Mark 1: 23 records, *"there was a man in their synagogue with an unclean spirit"*. In every instance the enemy presents himself in a place and manner that would not cause those who are his target alarm. He uses "good people" and "good places" to camouflage his true identity and objective. He depends on us not being able to detect his presence and activity until it is too late. He employs gradual compromise to bring us to a point of vulnerability and weakness.

Some of you may be wondering, *"Why is it necessary to recognize the enemy?"* The answer is your life depends on it. Your ability to detect the enemy's point of entry in our lives will not only affect the quality of our lives, but its quantity as well. You may not recognize the one thing that you've given place to in your life that is an agent of the enemy to keep you defeated, frustrated and broken. As long as it is allowed to stay, nothing will change.

Here are 10 ways to help you rightly appraise and discern the things that are presently part of your life, as well as those things you are considering allowing into to your life.

Ask yourself these questions:
62

J.C. MATTHEWS

1. *Does it draw you closer too and strengthen your relationship with God or does it draw attention to yourself?*
2. *Will it cause others to see Christ more clearly?*
3. *Is Jesus and the Kingdom of God glorified in your doing it?*
4. *Can it be supported biblically?*
5. *Is the benefit an enduring one or does it only satisfy an immediate need?*
6. *Is your life being enriched or depleted by it?*
7. *When speaking to others about it can you be nakedly honest regarding every detail and your involvement in or with it?*
8. *Do you have to rationalize its legitimacy in your life?*
9. *Do you have genuine God given peace in your spirit concerning your involvement or decision(s)?*
10. *Must you comprise God's Word or morality for it?*

By shining the light of God's Word and truth upon our lives we are now able to detect the enemies presence and position ourselves to wage a more victorious warfare!

J.C. MATTHEWS

What is God saying to me through this word?

_____

_____

_____

What adjustments or steps must I take to apply this word in my life?

_____

_____

_____

How has this word affected my approach to, and outlook upon, my life?

_____

_____

_____

Personal Notes & Thoughts:

_____

_____

_____

J.C. MATTHEWS

12

Jesus Makes the Difference

*"Observing the boldness of Peter and John and
realizing them to be uneducated and untrained
men, they were amazed and knew that they had
been with Jesus."*
(Acts 4:13, The Holman Christian Bible Version)

What *a powerful statement!* The religious elite, having
observed Peter and John's conduct and character, while
enduring persecution, said that they reminded them of Jesus.

Peter and John had just healed a man who was lame from
birth, preached until 5000 men came to Jesus, and immediately
thereafter, were thrown into jail on bogus charges. The

following morning they were brought before a court comprised of some of the same people who sent Jesus to the cross. In the face of this hostile situation, they stood boldly imbued with power of God. They did not speak until they were led by the Holy Spirit. They said what He told them to say, and did what He told them to do. They did not allow their flesh to give occasion to their accusers to find fault with them.

The Bible says that Peter and John's witness was so strong, that the one's who questioned them, after listening to them speak, *"had nothing to say in response."* (Acts 4:14). The ones who forcibly detained them had to set them free - untouched. Peter and John passed the test with flying colors. Their accusers where looking for a fight and end up seeing Jesus – *again!*

Often, when we are faced with conflict or volatile situations we allow our flesh to govern our conduct. We become part of the problem instead of allowing the Holy Spirit to guide us through our problem. We go to church on Sunday and leave Jesus at the door on our way out to face the remainder of the week. Jesus wants to come home with you. He wants to go to work with you. He wants to give you wisdom on how to talk to those who are trying to trap you. He wants to show you how to relate to those who despitefully use and don't appreciate you.

J.C. MATTHEWS

He wants to be the strength and wisdom you need to overcome what it is that has mounted an attack against you. However, you must let Him do the talking. The prophet Isaiah says that God: *"will keep him in perfect peace, whose mind is stayed on You, because he trusts in You"* (Isaiah 26:3-4, KJV).

Are you stressed out about a current or pending situation? How do you handle conflict and persecution? When you're going through what you go through, what do people see? Better yet – *"Who do they see?"* Is it you or Jesus? Stand in the power of His might. For *"greater is He that is in you than he that is in the world"* (1John 4:4). Remember, Jesus makes the difference!

Personal Meditations

What is God saying to me through this word?

_____

_____

_____

What adjustments or steps must I take to apply this word in my life?

_____

_____

_____

How has this word affected my approach to, and outlook upon, my life?

_____

_____

_____

Personal Notes & Thoughts:

_____

_____

_____

J.C. MATTHEWS

13

The Revelation in Separation

"And you shall remember that the Lord your God led you all the way these forty years in the wilderness, to humble you and test you, to know what was in your heart, whether you would keep His commandments or not. So He humbled you, allowed you to hunger, and fed you with manna which you did not know nor did your fathers know, that He might make you know that man shall not live by bread alone; but man lives by every word that proceeds from the mouth of the Lord" (Deut. 8:2-3 KJV).

I believe there are times in our lives when God removes us from the routine of life, and separates us from others, so that He can spend some time with us. Without God "taking this time" with us, we would drift through our lives preoccupied and distracted by life, never pursuing the destiny and purpose He created us for. Because these places of separation are often uncomfortable, we resist them and conclude that God must be punishing us, when in reality He is preparing us through separation. It is in these dry places, where no one else can help us (including ourselves), that we discover that God is our source, our healer and protector. We discover that our true source is not our jobs, families, education or money – but God alone! This level of revelation cannot be gained unless we have spent some quality time with God. Oftentimes, if we don't voluntarily *"make this time"* for God, He will involuntarily *"take this time"* for Himself.

Separation Is Often an Indication of Designation

If it seems like everyone and everything that you've always looked to for support is gone—it is not a coincidence but rather *divine providence.* It may be an indication that God is readying you for a transition in your life. Ask Abraham, the one whom God separated from his family to give him and his descendents a "Promised Land". Ask Joseph, the one who was forcibly removed from his father's house (of which he was the least of 12 brothers) so that he could become the second most powerful man in the world. Ask Moses, the one whom God separated from Egypt and prepared in the desert for 40 years to deliver

His people from slavery. Ask David, the youngest son of Jesse, the one whom King Saul removed from his father's house and placed in the palace where he could observe firsthand what it meant to be king. Finally, ask the apostle Paul, the one whom God separated from the pharisaical order so that he could become a leader and pillar in the Kingdom of God. Separation is an indication of God's designation of those He is calling.

Separation Is a Sign of Preparation

God is preparing and positioning you to discover something about Himself that He cannot reveal to you while you are surrounded by others. He needs to separate you from the people and things that you have placed in positions that belong to Him. They would only distract you from hearing and seeing the things He wants to show you. During this time of separation and seclusion, we also discover things about ourselves that we otherwise would have never known. There is no one to impress or save face with when we are alone. God has the ability to show us who we really are so that He can begin the process of molding us into who He's called us to be. God will remove our support and separate us from the things that we've become familiar with in order that He might reveal to us something much greater—Himself.

J.C. MATTHEWS

In Deuteronomy 8:2-3, we read that God purposefully led His people into the wilderness for the purpose of proving Himself to them. God used this place of isolation to develop their confidence in Him as their God. They did not labor for their living, they simply believed God and received their living. There was no Wal-Mart in the wilderness, therefore they had to trust God for their food, clothing and care. God proved to them that He was their one and only "true Source". They would have never received this revelation, without this time of separation and sanctification with God.

J.C. MATTHEWS

Personal Meditations

What is God saying to me through this word?

_____

_____

_____

What adjustments or steps must I take to apply this word in
my life?

_____

_____

_____

How has this word affected my approach to, and outlook upon,
my life?

_____

_____

_____

Personal Notes & Thoughts:

_____

_____

_____

J.C. MATTHEWS

14

Waiting on Something To Move

"Now there is at Jerusalem by the sheep market a pool, which is called in the Hebrew tongue Bethesda, having five porches. In these lay a great multitude of impotent folk, of blind, halt, withered, waiting for the moving of the water. And a certain man was there, which had an infirmity thirty and eight years."
John 5:2-5, KJV

I can remember driving home one night from work when I caught a flat tire. I didn't have a cell phone, flashlight or spare tire. There I was, on the side of the highway praying that someone would stop and help me get to a phone. I sat inside of my car with my flashers on for over three hours waiting for someone to stop. I will always remember the helpless feeling of being totally dependant upon the benevolence of a stranger. Finally, someone did stop and agreed to give me a ride to a phone. I was in his car for less than *5 minutes*. To my surprise, there was a payphone less than a half a mile away that I could have easily walked too. I waited hours for someone to do what I could've done for myself.

In the text, Jesus recognized a certain man who has been infirm for over 38 years. Jesus picked him out from a multitude of what the Bible describes as *"impotent folk"*. Maybe Jesus recognized him from the many years He and His parents would go to Jerusalem to observe the various feasts. Maybe, his specific condition was such that it drew attention to itself. However, I believe the reason Jesus singled him out from the crowd was Jesus saw something within the man that the man didn't see within himself. There are three lessons we must take from this text that will cause us to overcome the things that have kept us from experiencing wholeness in our lives.

First, this man's *infirmity had become his identity.* The Bible gives us his condition, but never gives us his name. We must be careful not to allow our problems, issues, situations or weaknesses to define who we are. It is possible for you to deal with something for so long that it begins to determine who you are and what you strive for in life. As a result, you lower your expectations and settle for much less than what God has planned for your life.

Secondly, *sometimes those around us fortify our infirmity.* Oftentimes, our immobility is in part due to the company we keep. People are more willing to tell you what you *can't* do as opposed to what you *can* do. They kill any dreams you may have of moving on by telling you all of the risks involved with the move, instead of encouraging you to take a leap of faith. The reason many of them do this is because they fear that you just may succeed at what they were afraid to attempt. Often, deliverance is found in doing what others around you have never done and risking the possibility of failure.

Finally, Jesus saw and knew his condition. Jesus knows exactly what you are going through and how long you've been going through it. He knows the desires of your heart and wants you to realize them. However, He allows us to experience the disappointment and frustration of relying on others to do what we must trust God to do. When this man's hope in others was exhausted God stepped in. Jesus did in a moment what he and others couldn't do over a 38 year period of time.

J.C. MATTHEWS

Are you waiting on something to move in your life before you attempt to achieve it? The Bible says this man waited 38 years for something to move, remaining in the same impotent condition. Jesus is saying the same thing to us He said to the man at the pool: "If you want to reach a dream or goal in your life, stop waiting on someone to help you achieve it – *"Get up and ... walk!*

Personal Meditations

What is God saying to me through this word?

_____

_____

_____

What adjustments or steps must I take to apply this word in
my life?

_____

_____

_____

How has this word affected my approach to, and outlook upon,
my life?

_____

_____

_____

Personal Notes & Thoughts:

_____

_____

_____

J.C. MATTHEWS

J.C. MATTHEWS

15

Redeeming The Time

"See then that you walk circumspectly, not as fools but as wise, redeeming the time, because the days are evil. Therefore do not be unwise, but understand what the will of the Lord is."
Ephesians 5:15-17

One of the most precious gifts God has given mankind is time. A major characteristic of time is that you will never have more of it than you have right now. With each breath you take, you are that much closer to taking your last breath. We all reach a point in life where we realize that we've lived more life than we have left. The older we become the more careful we are of what we spend our time doing and with whom we spend our time with. We begin to realize that we truly do not have *time to waste!*

Some of you may look over your shoulder at your past and smile with satisfaction at how you used the time that you've been given, while others may reflect on your past and wish that you had the ability to do some things all over again. However, what is done is done. We must do the best we can with the time we have left.

What do you do when you *now* have the *wisdom* to do a thing right, but you don't have the *time* to do it all over again? What do you do when opportunities, like water, have slipped through your fingers and the doors that were open are now shut? You may be asking: *"Is there any way to regain what I've lost over the years?"* The truth is, you will never be able to reclaim the time lost - but you may be able to *"redeem"* the time you have left!

The Bible instructs us to *"redeem the time"*. If we are instructed to redeem the time, the next question that must be asked is: *"How do we go about redeeming our time?"* The answer actually lies within the word *redeem*. The word *redeem* in the Greek is *"Exagorazo"*. It is a compound word made up of the preposition *"ex" which comes from "ek"* which is translated *"to come out of"* or *"from"*, and the verb *"Agorazo"*

82

which means *"to put to work in the marketplace"*. The marketplace is simply a system of exchange. The way to redeem your time is to exchange the system in which you are investing your time.

Many Believers, although born again by faith, still operate by a system dominated by the flesh. Anything that is not *logical* or *probable* they shy away from because they fear not being in control of the situation. They are operating under a system of *works*, which can only pay them *a wage*, which correspondingly controls their *worth*. This is the reason a person can work hard all their life and discover that the time they spent working was wasted because it could not give them what they earnestly desire – *freedom* and *fulfillment*.

God's system, or the Kingdom of God, is one of redemption that is founded on faith. Our productivity and worth is not based on our abilities or efforts, but our faith and obedience to God's Word. Everything we receive in this system is a gift. Jesus said, to seek first the Kingdom of God and His righteousness and all things will be added onto us (Matthew 6:33). God does what we can't do by our believing (in faith) that He can do it!

In the Bible, Abraham tried to have a son, under the system of flesh (or his own abilities and efforts) for almost 100 years without success. God gave Him in a moment, by faith, what he

83

J.C. MATTHEWS

could not produce by his flesh over a lifetime. God redeemed Abraham's time because Abraham switched systems. He received by faith what he could not produce by his flesh.

Like Abraham, God has allowed some of you to live long enough to know that your system doesn't work. God can fix in a moment what has been broken for years. It all depends on the system that you are investing your time and efforts in. It's not too late! Switch today and redeem your time!

J.C. MATTHEWS

What is God saying to me through this word?

_____

_____

_____

What adjustments or steps must I take to apply this word in my life?

_____

_____

_____

How has this word affected my approach to, and outlook upon, my life?

_____

_____

_____

Personal Notes & Thoughts:

_____

_____

_____

J.C. MATTHEWS

J.C. MATTHEWS

16

Surviving Dry Places

But He answered and said, "It is written, Man Shall
not live by bread alone, but on every word that
proceeds out of the mouth of God ".
Matthew 4:4, NASB

What does Deuteronomy 8:3 and Matthew 4:4 have in
common outside of them being almost identical in
wording? Of course, they are both found in the Bible. The
answer is: *They were both spoken in a wilderness or a dry*
place. Moses and Jesus both were concluding extended stays in
a wilderness and came to the same conclusion. Their
conclusion was: *"Man does not live by bread alone, but on*
every word that proceeds out of the mouth of God."

You may have never spent any period of time in an actual wilderness. However, at some point in your life you will find yourselves in some very dry places. Your dry place might be emotional, financial, physical, spiritual, relational or some other form of deficiency in your life. Each person's wilderness is just as real as the other's. These dry places and seasons in our lives are not designed to kill or stop us, but to grow us in our relationship and understanding of God. They are places of decision and learning where the flesh is tried and our spiritual man (or woman) is matured

The wilderness is not always a bad place. The purpose for the wilderness in our lives is three fold: (1) try us - physically, mentally and spiritually, (2) reveal ourselves to ourselves, (3) bring us to a place of total surrender to God. We must come to a place where we no longer seek fulfillment, meaning and sufficiency in others or our own efforts - but in God. Until we learn to trust God's Word in every situation we cannot enjoy the promises He has spoken over our lives.

I don't know what your particular wilderness is, but I can tell you that the test and the lesson is the same. God does not deny that you have needs. However, He does say that your primary means of meeting these needs should be found within His Word.

88

If you are currently in a "dry place" in your life ask yourself, "*What is it that God is trying to teach me here?*" "*Have I been depending on His Word or something or someone else?*" The answer to these questions may determine how long you'll be there. The children of Israel spent *40 years* in the wilderness before they entered into their promise because they continually failed the test. Jesus passed His test the first time and left His wilderness experience in *40 days.* The way to shorten your time in these dry places of life is to learn the lessons taught while there.

Personal Meditations

What is God saying to me through this word?

_____

_____

_____

What adjustments or steps must I take to apply this word in my life?

_____

_____

_____ \ _____

How has this word affected my approach to, and outlook upon, my life?

_____

_____

_____

Personal Notes & Thoughts:

_____

_____

_____

J.C. MATTHEWS

17

The Difference Between Being Lost and Being Led

"Then Moses led Israel from the Red Sea, and they went out into the wilderness."
Exodus 15:22

Many people who find themselves stuck in difficult situations often feel as if they've become lost. Somehow, they've arrived in a wilderness where everything has dried up and nothing seems to be growing. Many of them have lived in this wilderness for so long that they have given up on things changing and concluded that this must be all God has in store for them. On numerous occasions, they have attempted to change their situation, but all of their efforts have failed. If this sounds like you, you may not be lost at all! You may be squarely within the Will of God. All dry places in life are not the result of being lost. Sometimes God leads us into dry places and uses them as a place of preparation.

In Exodus 3:8, when God met Moses at the burning bush, He told him that He was going to deliver His people from bondage and into a land flowing with *"milk and honey"*. Yet, we know when God delivered His people from bondage, He *led them* directly into a *"wilderness"* where they spent 40 years. We know that their wilderness experience had a purpose because the Bible tells us that there was a shorter route available that they could have taken and avoided the wilderness altogether. Exodus 13:17 says, *"God did not <u>lead them</u> by the way of the land of the Philistines, even though it was near "(underline added).* Whenever God leads you somewhere He has a predetermined purpose for you, even if the route is longer than what you expected. The longer the preparation, the greater the promotion. It takes much longer to get a PhD than it does a GED. I am not putting down those who have a GED. Praise God for it. For some, it took just as much determination to get their GED than it did for others to obtain their PhD. However, we are speaking of principles.

Oftentimes, your wilderness is the doorway to your promise. At the initiation of Jesus' public ministry He was not led into

J.C. MATTHEWS

the temple, but into the wilderness. Jesus had to be first prepared in the wilderness before He could preach his first sermon.

If you are in a wilderness right now, remember what you learned while there because it will be necessary to sustain you in your Promised Land. Don't faint or lose heart. You may be at the door of your promise and purpose. I know it has been a long journey, but it will be worth your while. I know others may have arrived sooner at their place of destiny, and you are still making your way toward your destiny. What God wants to do in your life, requires preparation, therefore He had to take you the long way. There are no short cuts in the Kingdom of God – only God's way. I know, all the while you've thought that somehow you where lost. You may not have been lost at all. You just may have been *led!*

J.C. MATTHEWS

Personal Meditations

What is God saying to me through this word?

_____

_____

_____

What adjustments or steps must I take to apply this word in
my life?

_____

_____

_____

How has this word affected my approach to, and outlook upon,
my life?

_____

_____

_____

Personal Notes & Thoughts:

_____

_____

_____

J.C. MATTHEWS

18

The Deadly Deception

*"If you continue in My word, then you are truly
disciples of Mine; and you will know the truth, and the
truth will make you free." They answered Him, "We
are Abraham's descendants and have never yet been
enslaved to anyone; how is it that You say, `You will
become free'?" "If the Son makes you free, you will be
free indeed"* (John 8:31-36, NASB).

The deadliest deception in life is to go through it believing
you are *free*, when in fact you are really *bound!* If you
never realize you are bound, you will never fight for your
freedom. The tragedy in being bound and not knowing it is
that you never live the life God created you to live.

J.C. MATTHEWS

In the text, the Pharisees make a statement that reveals their true condition – *bound*. They tell Jesus that they are: *"Abraham's descendants and have never yet been enslaved to anyone"*. The Bible is clear in that, throughout the Nation of Israel's history they were at various times enslaved (Egyptians, Philistines and the Babylonians). As a matter of fact, they where presently under the Roman Empire's rule. They had become so accustomed to being in bondage that their bondage appeared to them to be freedom. It is possible for you to become so familiar with a situation (no matter how dysfunctional, painful or out of order it may be) that it becomes the standard by which you measure life. What is bondage to one person may be freedom to another. Our perception of life can become skewed by our circumstances. *Self-deception* is the precursor to *self-destruction*.

Paul warns in 2 Corinthians 2:11, *"so that no advantage would be taken of us by Satan, ... we should not be ignorant of his schemes.* The enemy's primary mode of operation is deception. He offers us a counterfeit of true freedom, hoping that we will embrace the substitute never having experienced the real thing. Much of the fruitlessness in the lives of Believers today is a result of unidentified bondages. Bondage does not have to painful to be bondage. As a matter of fact, the worse kind of bondage is bondage that you've become

96

comfortable with. You can recognize bondage if it hinders your ability to experience the fellowship, fullness and freedom that God has planned for your life.

Jesus said, *"the truth will set you free"*. Take a moment, get away from everybody and everything, close your eyes and ask God to reveal to you anything that is hidden in your heart and life that has caused you to operate in self-deception. Allow the light of His Word to illuminate your life and path. Let this be the beginning of a new chapter in your life. Discover the freedom and fullness of living transparently and you will really know what it means to truly be *free indeed!*

J.C. MATTHEWS

Personal Meditations

What is God saying to me through this word?

_____

_____

_____

What adjustments or steps must I take to apply this word in my life?

_____

_____

_____

How has this word affected my approach to, and outlook upon, my life?

_____

_____

_____

Personal Notes & Thoughts:

_____

_____

_____

J.C. MATTHEWS

19

God's Waiting Room

"I would have lost heart, unless I had believed that I would see the goodness of the Lord In the land of the living. Wait on the Lord; Be of good courage, And He shall strengthen your heart; Wait, I say, on the Lord!" (Psalms 27:13-14, NKJV).

Fainting is a consequence of *waiting* while *fearful* accompanied by an absence of *hope*. One of the most nerve wrecking and unpleasant experiences one can have in life is having to wait on something.

God has a *"waiting room"* that He uses to prepare us not to punish us. While waiting on God, we are not sitting around idle *waiting* on something to happen. We are to make it happen. When the bible speaks of "waiting" on God, it is referencing our assumption of a servant's disposition. To illustrate this point, consider when you go out for dinner. Upon being seated you will generally be greeted by someone identified as your waiter. The waiter's job is to serve you and make sure that your needs are met during your stay. We would be shocked if our waiter went and had a seat, never returning to the table to see if our needs were met. We would not say that he waited on us at all, and the absence of a tip would reflect his lack of service.

While we are waiting on God, we should be working to prepare ourselves for a greater revelation of Him by serving Him. When we are prepared, God will reward us for our faithfulness and release to us what He has been preparing us for. The worst thing that can happen is to receive what you've been asking for and ruin it because you weren't prepared for it.

What makes waiting so difficult is that we generally have a need, or are in a situation, in which we need help, but it is nowhere to be found. Therefore, the power of the situation increases as we become disheartened and fearful of *negative possibilities*. Fear is our receiving negative possibilities as if they were present realities.

J.C. MATTHEWS

The unknown has caused more people to faint in life than those things that actually come to pass. The reason for this is, we generally think negatively when it comes to possibilities. Many are suffering unnecessarily from depression and other negative emotions because they have allowed a situation that has not *materialized* to be *realized.* This is *counter faith.* They are exercising faith in reverse. "*Faith is the substance of things hoped for the evidence of things not seen*" (Hebrews 11:1, KJV). Biblical faith that comes from God speaks of hope! Your hope of a positive outcome is what gives you the strength to endure these temporary situations.

If Biblical faith is of God, then counter faith is of the enemy. It is the enemy's way of getting you to forfeit the possibilities of a better tomorrow by having you live out today that which may never happen. David says that God will *strengthen* you during your time of waiting. When you leave His waiting room you will be stronger than when you entered. God's waiting room may not be a pleasant place, but it is a necessary place.

> *Wait on the Lord; Be of good courage, And He shall strengthen your heart; Wait, I say, on the Lord!"*

J.C. MATTHEWS

Personal Meditations

What is God saying to me through this word?

_____

_____

_____

What adjustments or steps must I take to apply this word in
my life?

_____

_____

_____

How has this word affected my approach to, and outlook upon,
my life?

_____

_____

_____

Personal Notes & Thoughts:

_____

_____

_____

J.C. MATTHEWS

20

Do You Believe He is Able?

"He entered the house, the blind men came up to Him, and Jesus said to them, "Do you believe that I am able to do this?"
Matthew 9:28, NASB

Have you ever read the Bible and wondered why Jesus would ask a blind or lame man if they wanted to be healed before He healed them? The Bible says in John 5:6, that Jesus saw a man who had been crippled for 38 years lying next to a pool and asked him, *"Do you wish to get well?"* More specifically, in Matthew 9:28 the bible says, *"He (Jesus) entered the house, the blind men came up to Him, and Jesus said to them, "Do you believe that I am able to do this?"* The reason Jesus ask these needy individuals these seemingly obvious questions, is because Jesus understood that there is a real connection between what we *"believe"* and what we *"receive"*. Jesus knew that they first must *believe* that they could be delivered before they were able to receive deliverance. It is possible for someone to have been in a condition for so long that they refuse to believe that anyone can help them. For God to change many of our situations we must first believe that things can be better, and that better is God's will for our lives.

In Romans 4:3, we are given the secret to the blessing Abraham enjoyed in his life. The text says, *"Abraham believed God and it was credited to him as righteousness."* The secret is simply - Abraham *"believed God".* As a matter of fact, God granted him the desire of his heart, not because he was perfect and obeyed His every command, but because he believed Him. Abraham didn't earn what God gave him, he simply believed God for what he could not do in his own power. Your ability to believe in God's goodness and His predetermined purpose for your life is what gives you the ability to exceed your limitations. The Bible says that Abraham believed God despite living in an objectively dead situation. His belief in God's goodness above the deadness of his situation is what gave birth to his blessing.

J.C. MATTHEWS

Belief that life has something better in store for you is what will empower you to overcome what otherwise has overcome you. The reason so many people's situation becomes their destination is because they believe that their situation can't change. What we believe is the most important and determinative factor in our lives. What we believe will determine what we strive to accomplish and what we will settle for. Believing in something gives it life and makes it a reality in our lives.

What is it that you need or want to change in your life? In order to see better, you must believe better. Better is available, but you have to believe that it is God's will for your life and that it is available. Just as we saw above, Jesus is asking you the same question He asked the blind men in the text, *"Do you believe that I am able to do this?"*

Personal Meditations

What is God saying to me through this word?

_____

_____

_____

What adjustments or steps must I take to apply this word in my life?

_____

_____

_____

How has this word affected my approach to, and outlook upon, my life?

_____

_____

_____

Personal Notes & Thoughts:

_____

_____

_____

J.C. MATTHEWS

21

You Must First "Be" What You Hope To Become

"Neither shall thy name any more be called Abram,
but thy name shall be Abraham; for a father of many
nations have I made thee."
Genesis 17:4-5, KJV

I can remember when I began to write my first book. I felt as if God was leading me to do it, but I wasn't sure of how to start. I had never written a book before and did not personally know anyone who had done so themselves. As I considered actually doing it, doubt and fear ran through my mind saying, *"No one knows who you are. What do you have to say that hasn't already been said? Who do you think you are?* As these thoughts went through my mind, I heard God say, *"I'll tell you who you are, - you are an "author". Now get started writing!"*

At that moment I realized something that revolutionized the way in which I approached achieving the things in life I hoped to achieve. I realized, in order to become an author I had to first do what authors do. I had to first write. If I had waited for someone to declare me an author before I began writing, I would have never authored my first book. As part of my ''being" what I was seeking to "become", I began to read as much as I could about the publishing process. I went to industry events that authors frequented, so I could familiarize myself with that environment. I had to "be it" before I could ever "become it".

There are some promises and opportunities in life you cannot afford to wait until they present themselves to begin the process of preparing for them. You must be ready for your moment when it comes. You must become so pregnant and possessed with your promise that when your moment comes you are able and ready to deliver. You must position and prepare yourself to operate at the level you intend to occupy before you actually occupy it. If you practice being what you hope to become, when the opportunity arises, you won't be intimidated by it because you have already prepared for it.

J.C. MATTHEWS

So many people fail to realize what they hope for because they believe that they must wait until everything is in place before they attempt to accomplish anything. They want all of their resources and support in place first and leave no room for faith in God. Because this ideal rarely materializes, they allow their hopes to go unrealized and are unprepared for the opportunities that do present themselves.

This is backwards. In the Kingdom of God "we walk by faith and not by sight" (2 Corinthians. 5:7). "Faith is the substance of things hoped for and the evidence of things not seen" (Hebrews 11:1). Anything that God places in your heart to accomplish you already possess the substance necessary to cause it to manifest in your life. You must believe that whatever God has promised you already exists and is yours before you actually possess it. Just because you can't see it (yet) doesn't mean it doesn't exist. If God said it – it's already done!

Oftentimes in the Bible, when God spoke a promise concerning a person He spoke it in the past tense. When God told Abraham that his name would no longer be "Abram" but "Abraham", because He *had made him* the father of many nations, Abraham was still childless! Did God lie? Never! God was simply revealing to him what He had already done. In order for

Abraham to receive his promise he had to operate within his promise. Every time Sarah called him "Abraham" he was reminded of who God had made him - the "father of many nations".

What is it that you are hoping will manifest in your life? You must be what you're becoming because transformation is the precursor to manifestation.

Personal Meditations

What is God saying to me through this word?

_____

_____

_____

What adjustments or steps must I take to apply this word in my life?

_____

_____

_____

How has this word affected my approach to, and outlook upon, my life?

_____

_____

_____

Personal Notes & Thoughts:

_____

_____

_____

J.C. MATTHEWS

J.C. MATTHEWS

22

A Fixed Fight

*"Do not fear or be dismayed because of this great
multitude, for the battle is not yours but God's ... 'You
need not fight in this battle; station yourselves, stand
and see the salvation of the LORD on your behalf, O
Judah and Jerusalem.' Do not fear or be dismayed;
tomorrow go out to face them, for the LORD is with
you"* (2 Chronicles 20:15-17, NASB).

If you are a boxing fan, you are familiar with the statement:
"the fight was fixed". If there was ever a fixed fight, the
one in 2 Chronicles 20 was just that. Three nations, that God
forbade the nation of Israel from destroying earlier, has now
come together to destroy them. The Bible records the Nation
of Israel saying to God:

J.C. MATTHEWS

"Now behold, the sons of Ammon and Moab and Mount Seir, whom You did not let Israel invade when they came out of the land of Egypt (they turned aside from them and did not destroy them), see how they are rewarding us by coming to drive us out from Your possession which You have given us as an inheritance"

(2 Chronicles 20:10-11).

Unbeknownst to the Nation of Israel, God was using these nations to serve a higher purpose. This seemingly impossible situation was orchestrated by God to: (1) demonstrate to Israel that He was able to care for them, no matter how severe their situation seemed, and (2) that their ability was not determinative of their success, but their faith in Him. God allowed Israel's problem to grow until it was out of their control. Now they stood face to face with a situation that they could no longer avoid. This situation was not to destroy them but to teach them, that the battle is not theirs, but the Lords.

Many of you may be facing situations in your life that seem to have come out of nowhere, when in reality they are old problems that have re-surfaced. This problem seems to be unavoidable and insurmountable. You've thought about and considered every scenario, trying to find a way of escape and delivery but none have been revealed. You've prayed to God about it but He seems to have turned a deaf ear to your prayer.

J.C. MATTHEWS

Now it appears that you are on the brink of losing everything. Just remember, that God did not allow the problem in your life to destroy you but to develop your faith in Him. He already knows how you are going to win. *The fight has been fixed! Weeping may endure for a night, but joy is coming in the morning! (Psalms 30:5).*

This problem is only temporary. God never intended for you to have to fight this fight. It is too big for you. God has allowed the situation to get to this point to reveal to you that: (1) no problem is too big for Him, (2) you are never alone, even when it seems like it, and (3) that the fight is really His. Understand, that the decisive factor in your success is not "what" has come against you - but *Who* is with you. Remember, it may look like you are insufficient, out numbered and unable to overcome what is facing you. In the natural this might be true if it was up to you alone. However, the battle is not yours but the Lords.

Before the battle ever begins, God has already declared you delivered and victorious. Your fight is not against the problem, but yourself. You must fight to hold onto your faith in God, even when the facts contradict what God has promised. Remember, facts change everyday, but the truth of God's word never changes regardless of the facts. When your opponent or

115

J.C. MATTHEWS

problem rises up against you, it is already defeated. The fight has been fixed – it just hasn't be made aware of this truth yet!

J.C. MATTHEWS

Personal Meditations

What is God saying to me through this word?

_____

_____

_____

What adjustments or steps must I take to apply this word in my life?

_____

_____

_____

How has this word affected my approach to, and outlook upon, my life?

_____

_____

_____

Personal Notes & Thoughts:

_____

_____

_____

J.C. MATTHEWS

J.C. MATTHEWS

23

God's Opportunities

"Because you have relied on the king of Syria, and have not relied on the Lord your God, therefore the army of the king of Syria has escaped from your hand. Were the Ethiopians and the Lubim not a huge army with very many chariots and horsemen? Yet, because you relied on the Lord, He delivered them into your hand. For the eyes of the Lord run to and fro throughout the whole earth, to show Himself strong on behalf of those whose heart is loyal to Him.". And in the thirty-ninth year of his reign, Asa became diseased in his feet, and his malady was severe; yet in his disease he did not seek the Lord, but the physicians."
2 Chronicles 16:7-9, 12-13 (NKJV)

J.C. MATTHEWS

Have you been robbing God of the opportunity to be glorified in your life? Much of the frustration we face in life is really our denying God the opportunity to demonstrate Himself able to handle the problems that are too great for us. When we place our confidence in men and turn to others for help, instead of God, we deny Him the opportunity to be glorified. Our problems are really open invitations for God's participation in our lives. Everyday, people suffer unnecessarily because they deny God the opportunity to get involved in their lives and thereby be glorified

King Asa made a similar mistake when he placed his confidence in man, instead of God. God gave King Asa not only victory, but also unusual peace, despite the fact he was surrounded by hostile nations. The Bible records that King Asa became sick and he once again placed his confidence and his life in the hands of men instead of calling upon God for his healing. As a result, he not only lost God's blessing over his life, but his life itself.

How often, do we decide to turn from God, who has already proven Himself faithful, able and willing to see us through our struggles? It was God who has kept us from being totally destroyed by our enemies - seen and unseen. He has hid us and

J.C. MATTHEWS

not allowed our adversaries to know when we are weak, nor has he exposed our hidden faults.

What is it in your life that God is waiting for you to turn over to Him and give Him the opportunity to show Himself strong? Your *impossibilities* are really *God's opportunities*. When you deprive Him of the opportunity to demonstrate His sovereignty you also deprive Him of glory that is due Him. When you need help, don't look around – but look up! David, facing a seemingly impossible situation, asked himself a question and came to the right conclusion. David said, *"I will lift up my eyes to the mountains; from where shall my help come? My help comes from the LORD, Who made heaven and earth"* (Psalms 121:1-2, NASB). Remember, the impossibility you are facing might actually be an opportunity for God to show Himself strong!

J.C. MATTHEWS

Personal Meditations

What is God saying to me through this word?

_____
_____
_____

What adjustments or steps must I take to apply this word in my life?

_____
_____
_____

How has this word affected my approach to, and outlook upon, my life?

_____
_____
_____

Personal Notes & Thoughts:

_____
_____
_____

J.C. MATTHEWS

24

Learning How To Avoid Making Bad Decisions

"One day when Jacob was cooking some stew, Esau arrived home exhausted and hungry from a hunt. Esau said to Jacob, "I'm starved! Give me some of that red stew you've made." (This was how Esau got his other name, Edom - "Red.") Jacob replied, "All right, but trade me your birthright for it." "Look, I'm dying of starvation!" said Esau. "What good is my birthright to me now?" So Jacob insisted, "Well then, swear to me right now that it is mine." So Esau swore an oath, thereby selling all his rights as the firstborn to his younger brother. Then Jacob gave Esau some bread and lentil stew. Esau ate and drank and went on about his business, indifferent to the fact that he had given up his birthright" (Genesis 25:29-34, NLT).

How many of you have made bad decisions in your life? It may have been five, ten or even twenty years ago and you are still paying for them. A decision that took only moments to make ends up costing you years of your life trying to recover from it. It may have been a financial, marital, relational or occupational decision that has shaped your world as it exists today. One thing is for sure: If you knew then, what you know now, you would have chosen differently. For some of you, one bad decision has kept you from experiencing the fullness of the purpose that God has for you in your life. However, bad decisions do not have to be *fatal* – they can also be *formative*.

One of the most difficult but necessary skills we must develop in life is how to make decisions. When we make the *best decisions,* we <u>gain</u> ground. When we make *good decisions*, we <u>maintain</u> ground. However, when we make *bad decisions,* we lose ground and oftentimes much more. There is no formula that can be applied to every situation that will enable us to avoid making bad decisions. However, the Bible does contain principles that can be applied to our situations to enable us to make the best decisions possible considering our circumstances.

In Genesis chapter 25, the Bible presents us with a situation in which Esau makes a bad decision. Not only does his decision impact his life, but the lives of generations to come. If Esau where here today, I believe he would give the following advise:

1. **Never make a decision while needy.** *"Esau arrived home exhausted and hungry from a hunt. Esau said to Jacob, "I'm starved! Give me some of that red stew you've made"* (verse 29-30).

A man could sell a thirsty man a glass of water for all he owns. This actually happened when Joseph was placed over Egypt during the great famine. People came from far and near giving him all their money, land and the right to 20% of their future produce. "Need" clouds our vision and ability to make sound decisions. Whenever we make decisions in the midst of a crisis, or ones that are based on need, it will more than likely be *shortsighted* decisions and will end up costing us disproportionately more than what we received.

2. **Never allow anyone to make you decide "now" on something that can wait.** *"Jacob replied, "All right, but trade me your birthright for it."* (verse 31).

There are very few decisions in life that need to be made *right now on the spot.* Often, by waiting and praying prior to making a decision, we can more fully take into consideration the totality of our situation and the consequences of making the decision. If someone tries to pressure you into making a decision right now about something that doesn't require an immediate decision, you will more than likely regret the decision.

3. **Avoid empowering or exaggerating your need.** *"Jacob replied, "All right, but trade me your birthright for it." "Look, I'm dying of starvation!" said Esau. "What good is my birthright to me now?"*

Often, we become victim to pressure because we exaggerate or create a need that does not exist. Esau was not dying - he was merely hungry. His exaggerated perception of his situation, paved the way for him to lose what was most valuable to him. We know that the birthright was important to him because in the Book of Hebrews we are told that he sought after it with great weeping (Hebrews 12:17).

4. **Never exchange something enduring for something temporary.** *"Then Jacob gave Esau some bread and lentil stew. Esau ate and drank and went on about his business, indifferent to the fact that he had given up his birthright"*

126

When Esau finished eating his stew, the fact remained, that he would become hungry again, but Jacob now owned an enduring blessing and birthright. Decisions that are made based on your flesh will more than likely be bad ones. These decisions generally momentarily satisfy, but have long-term consequences.

Short sighted and quick decisions are a major means by which the enemy robs Believers of the blessings that God places in our lives. Since God has given you authority over the enemy and his kingdom, he must convince you to *give him* what he *cannot take*. He's been using the same trick from the very beginning. It was a bad decision that caused Adam and Eve to fall in the garden. Satan offered them a piece of fruit for something eternal.

You may be struggling to overcome the consequences of bad decisions made in your past and wondering how you can stop paying interest on something that happened years ago. The answer is - by making good, better and the best decisions now. It was a good decision you made to accept Christ as your Savior that empowered you to overcome the death sentence Adam delivered to us all by his fall. Make better decisions today and experience all God has planned for your tomorrow!

J.C. MATTHEWS

Personal Meditations

What is God saying to me through this word?

_____

_____

_____

What adjustments or steps must I take to apply this word in
my life?

_____

_____

_____

How has this word affected my approach to, and outlook upon,
my life?

_____

_____

_____

Personal Notes & Thoughts:

_____

_____

_____

J.C. MATTHEWS

J.C. MATTHEWS

25

How Long?

"And He asked his father, "How long has this been happening to him?" And he said, "From childhood. "It has often thrown him both into the fire and into the water to destroy him but if You can do anything, take pity on us and help us!" And Jesus said to him, " `If You can?' All things are possible to him who believes." Immediately the boy's father cried out and said, "I do believe; help my unbelief" (Mark 9:21-24, NASB).

In this text, Jesus asks a timeless question that is just as relevant today as it was the day it was spoken. Whenever you read that Jesus asked a question, it is a teaching moment. He never asks questions because He doesn't know the answer or for edification. For Jesus knows what is in the hearts of

J.C. MATTHEWS

men. Whenever Jesus asks a question, He is not only speaking to the individual before Him, but to those who would subsequently read the account.

Jesus, after coming down from the mountain, is immediately presented with a situation. He is met by a father who has a demon-possessed son. This is not something that has recently come about, but is something that he has been living with for years. It is a persistent problem. A problem that has not become better but has grown worse over time. A problem that he was able to hide in his home for a while, but has grown to the point that it has spilled over into his public life. Now the problem has taken over and he is no longer able to control it. It shows up at the most inopportune times. It now affects his relationships and his ability to live and enjoy life. He has become a captive of this issue in his life. Jesus seeing this man asks a question that appears simple, but is the key to the man and his son's deliverance.

Jesus, the God-Man, who knows the beginning from the end, asks: *"How long has this been happening...?"* It was a question designed to cause the man to reflect on his situation. How long have you been living with this dysfunction, disorder, habit or issue in your life? How long have you been putting up with this issue that you should have cast out along time ago?

132

How long have you been tolerating its presence and accepting less than what God has for you in your life? How long have you allowed this situation to fester? Jesus is asking you and I the same question.

You can live with a situation so long that dysfunction becomes normal and sin becomes acceptable. Suffering becomes routine and disappointment is now expected. Things that you would originally have cast out and cast away a long time ago, you now tolerate.

In Jesus' question *"How long"*, he illuminates the path to deliverance for the father's son and for us as well. This question causes us not only to look back at the origin of our issue(s) or situation(s), but the reason why they remain an issue, and how we can prevent them from continuing in our lives.

The **first step** toward deliverance is *recognition*. The question, *'How long?"*, was designed to cause the man to reflect upon his situation. To cause him to identify the origin of his problem. How did it begin and how did it get to the place it is today? It is important for us to understand and identify the source and origin of our pain, before we attempt to deal with it. If you don't identify its origin, you may only be treating a symptom and not the source.

133

J.C. MATTHEWS

Secondly, the question also insinuates that this was something the father had control over. I believe that Jesus was really asking him, "How long have you been willing to tolerate this situation?" There are some things in life that God has given us the power and responsibility of handling ourselves. We pray and seek others to help us with our issues, when the answer and power to deal with them, has already been given to us.

Thirdly, you must believe that things can change. The reason this problem became a persistent one is found in Jesus' statement to the father that, *"All things are possible to him who believes."* Many of our situations don't change because we've lived with them for so long, that we no longer believe or expect them to change. What you believe matters the most. Jesus did what the father should have been able to do. You may be dealing with or tolerating a situation that seems impossible. It has become an impossibility because you have given up on believing that it can change. You must believe that you deserve better. You must believe that the rest of your life will be better than the life you have already lived.

You have the power to make a change that will not only affect your life but also the lives of those you love. Your belief that deliverance and breakthrough in your life is possible will determine *"how long"* you must endure you current situation.

134

Jesus said, *"All things are possible to him who believes."* This includes you too!

J.C. MATTHEWS

Personal Meditations

What is God saying to me through this word?

_____

_____

_____

What adjustments or steps must I take to apply this word in my life?

_____

_____

_____

How has this word affected my approach to, and outlook upon, my life?

_____

_____

_____

Personal Notes & Thoughts:

_____

_____

_____

J.C. MATTHEWS

26

Underestimating Your Anointing

"Now a certain woman of the wives of the sons of the prophets cried out to Elisha, "Your servant my husband is dead, and you know that your servant feared the LORD; and the creditor has come to take my two children to be his slaves." Elisha said to her, "What shall I do for you? Tell me, what do you have in the house?" And she said, "Your maidservant has nothing in the house except a jar of oil" (2 Kings 4:1-2, NASB).

In meditating on this scripture, I believe the man of God knew that this widow had something in her house more valuable than what she was looking to receive from him. The only problem was – she didn't know it!

J.C. MATTHEWS

Throughout the Bible oil is representative of *anointing*. It represents the presence and power of the Holy Spirit upon a person or vessel. The Bible says that her husband served the man of God and feared the Lord. This was an *anointed man*. For years an anointing rested in their home. The man of God knew as long as there was anointing in the house everything she needed was likewise in the house. She was looking for money when God had given her something greater – an anointing. Money is the least of God's blessings. As long as our focus is on money we will miss out on what God, through His anointing, can do in our lives. As a matter of fact, the anointing will cause money to show up when it is activated in a situation. When we begin to operate in our anointing, we have God's presence and power accompanying our efforts. With God all things are possible.

Every Believer is anointed and carries within them the very same Holy Spirit Jesus Christ (The Anointed One) had upon Him. Like the jar of oil that sat on the widow's shelf overlooked and underestimated, many of us have done the same thing to the anointing that is present in our lives. We turn to people and other tangible things for answers, when God has already placed the answer within us, in the form of His Holy Spirit. The Bible describes the Holy Spirit as a Comforter, Guide, Teacher and Revealer. He has the answer to what

138

perplexes us. In many cases, we don't need more money - we need revelation of our situation. We need discernment, enlightenment and direction to make a right decision. If we were to give the Holy Spirit free course in our lives, He would show us the abundance that God has already placed within us; but has thus far gone overlooked and underestimated.

The Holy Spirit wants to give you life in every respect of the word. If there is anything dead, unfruitful or dying in our lives, we must give the Holy Spirit access to it, so that He can breathe upon it the breath of life. The anointing, represents the presence of the Holy Spirit, and was given so that we could experience life to its fullest. He can out produce anything, anyone or any system anywhere. However, we must trust Him!

Never underestimate your anointing. It is God's most precious provision for us to prosper in our lives. It is the *anointing* that breaks the yoke of bondage and causes us to overcome our situations – whatever our situations may be!

> *"And it shall come to pass in that day, that his burden shall be taken away from off thy shoulder, and his yoke from off thy neck, and the yoke shall be destroyed because of the anointing"* (Isaiah 10:27, KJV).

139

J.C. MATTHEWS

Personal Meditations

What is God saying to me through this word?

_____

_____

_____

What adjustments or steps must I take to apply this word in
my life?

_____

_____

_____

How has this word affected my approach to, and outlook upon,
my life?

_____

_____

_____

Personal Notes & Thoughts:

_____

_____

_____

J.C. MATTHEWS

27

All My Help

"I will lift up my eyes to the mountains; From where shall my help come? My help comes from the LORD, Who made heaven and earth."
Psalms 121:1-2, NASB

As I watched television and witnessed the suffering caused by Hurricane Katrina, the Lord revealed to me a truth that I, and we as a nation, should never forget.

We watched in disbelief as thousands of people slept on rooftops, mothers and their children going days without food or another change of clothes, while dead bodies and what used to

J.C. MATTHEWS

be peoples' homes and belongings where scattered about the streets like rubbish. There was no food, no medicine, no water and no order. Days passed with no visible sign of law enforcement in one of the nations largest cities. As the news cameras drove by, people cried out something that spoke to my spirit. Their cry revealed a deeper problem than what their words communicated and had a common theme. They were all looking for *help!!!"*

Many people around the world are wondering, how could people in the wealthiest nation on earth be left in such a condition. The answer is in where we have sought our help. Since September 11th, America has formed FEMA and the Homeland Security agencies, bolstered the military's budget and membership, passed laws and erected metal detectors in an effort to make America a more secure place.

Their cry for help was more than a plea for water or food, but something greater. They will drink the water provided and will thirst again. They will consume the food donated and will need a meal tomorrow. The government failed them and no man could truly deliver them from their situation. The truth of the matter is, there are some problems in life that neither the pen nor the pocketbook can fix. There are threats, just as real as someone strapped with explosives, that can't be detected or detained by heightened security.

As Hurricane Katrina proved, there are problems in life require us to turn to *true Sovereignty for our protection and provision!* Through our vast array of technology, we expected and watched her coming, but could do nothing to protect ourselves from her fury.

Hurricane Katrina reminded and revealed something to America and the world that we must never forget. We may not be going through a hurricane, but the way in which we get through and overcome it is the same. The Psalmist wrote: "*Unless the LORD guards the city, the watchman keeps awake in vain.*" (Psalms 127:1, NASB). Anything that we entrust our hope and security in that does not begin and include God is destined to fail.

I believe that the men, women and children that we saw crying out for *"help"* was a universal cry for all mankind. This cry is really a question: *"Who can we really trust?"* David asked a similar question when confronted with destruction, but came to the right conclusion when he wrote:

J.C. MATTHEWS

*" I will lift up my eyes to the mountains; From
where shall my help come? My help {comes}
from the LORD, Who made heaven and earth."*
(Psalms 121:1-2)

J.C. MATTHEWS

Personal Meditations

What is God saying to me through this word?

_____

_____

_____

What adjustments or steps must I take to apply this word in
my life?

_____

_____

_____

How has this word affected my approach to, and outlook upon,
my life?

_____

_____

_____

Personal Notes & Thoughts:

_____

_____

_____

J.C. MATTHEWS

J.C. MATTHEWS

28

The Breaking in Your Breakthrough

"Elisha sent a messenger to him, saying, " Go and wash in the Jordan seven times, and your flesh will be restored to you and you will be clean." But Naaman was furious and went away and said, "Behold, I thought, 'He will surely come out to me and stand and call on the name of the LORD his God, and wave his hand over the place and cure the leper.' "Are not Abanah and Pharpar, the rivers of Damascus, better than all the waters of Israel? Could I not wash in them and be clean?" So he turned and went away in a rage" (2 Kings 5:10-12,NASB).

J.C. MATTHEWS

Often, the greatest obstacle to our experiencing the blessing of God in our lives is ourselves!

When I was a sophomore in High School I asked my Dad to buy me a car so I could drive to school instead of catching the bus. I didn't think this would be a problem because he always bragged about the car he had when he was a sophomore in High School. To my surprise my Dad said, "No". I asked him why, and he said, *"Because you need a job first."* He arranged an interview for me with a local bowling alley where he bowled every weekend. To my surprise, my job consisted of picking up trash from the parking lot. I couldn't believe it! Every Saturday morning I got up early and walked the parking lot with a broom and a poker stick (for trash), all the while pulling a humungous trashcan on wheels. On a few occasions some of my *"friends"* from school came by and taunted me while I worked. I was devastated.

After several months of this I was just about to quit when I received the surprise of my life. One morning, my father picked me up after work and took me to a car lot where he purchased my first car. When I got home I asked him, "Why he bought me the car? My Dad looked me in the eyes and said, *"Jimmy, it was always my intention to get you the car, but I had to be sure that you had the character to handle such a responsibility. You*

148

needed to learn the value of money and to know how much value to place on other people's opinion of you. I figured if you can stick it out at the bowling alley and not quit with the razzing you received from your friends, then I could trust you to make the right decision when you're with your friends and outside of my presence."

The Bible declares, *"My thoughts are not your thoughts, nor are your ways My ways," declares the LORD. "My ways higher than your ways and My thoughts than your thoughts"* (Isaiah 55:8-9). God has the benefit of being omniscient (knowing all things) and omnipotent (having all power). He knows the beginning and the end of a matter. He knows how to perfectly bless us. His timing is perfect. His proportion is perfect. The level at which He blesses us is perfect for the level we occupy. There are considerations that we are not aware of that can greatly complicate our ability to properly enjoy, handle and receive what we've ask God for.

As I look at this text, God demonstrates the same principle my father taught me in High School, through Naaman's situation. Naaman suffered from pride. God wanted to first do something on the inside of Naaman that would prepare him to receive what God would later do on the outside. He was a high-ranking official in the Aramean army and thought what God asked him

J.C. MATTHEWS

to do was beneath Him. In order for God to move on our behalf, we must move out of His way. When Naaman asked the man of God to bless him, God had to first break him. The man of God told this diplomat to humble himself and dip in the muddy Jordan River seven times to receive his healing. At first, Naaman refused and said to his maid, that he thought that the man of God would do something dignified and heal him. But God had to break his pride so that he could receive his healing. When Naaman humbled himself and did as he was instructed, the healing took place immediately. This principle is critical to our experiencing breakthrough in our lives.

What is it that you've asked God to do for you? What is it that God has asked you do first? There is a greater blessing and revelation for you in obeying God than merely receiving His blessing! God prefers broken vessels. There are some breakthroughs that won't happen in your life until you've been broken!

Personal Meditations

What is God saying to me through this word?

_____

_____

_____

What adjustments or steps must I take to apply this word in my life?

_____

_____

_____

How has this word affected my approach to, and outlook upon, my life?

_____

_____

_____

Personal Notes & Thoughts:

_____

_____

_____

J.C. MATTHEWS

J.C. MATTHEWS

29

The Making in The Shaking

*"So I prophesied as I was commanded; and as I
prophesied, there was a noise, and behold, a
rattling; and the bones came together, bone to its
bone"* (Ezekiel 37:7, NASB).

If we live long enough, there will be something that happens
in our lives that shakes us, causing us to re-examine our
lives and what we are living for. It renders us motionless and
causes thoughts of desperation and uncertainty to fill our
minds. What is even more disturbing is that they often come
unannounced.

These events are what I call *destiny points*. They are points in life where you must make decisions concerning your life that will chart the course for the rest of your life. What makes these decisions so difficult is that we must often make them in the midst of a crisis. However, we must learn not to allow our *crisis* to determine the *quality* of our decisions. There are ways in which the shock and intimidation of our circumstances can be minimized thereby allowing us to properly perceive our situation and make sober decisions. To do this we must gain understanding. Let's take a look Ezekiel and how he handled the shaking he experienced.

The prophet Ezekiel was literally caught by surprise by a sudden shaking in his life. He did nothing wrong to cause the shaking. As a matter of fact, he was doing what God told him to do.

Understanding No. One:
All trials in life are not the result of wrongdoing or punishment. God told Ezekiel to speak to his dry situation - and he did. Ezekiel obeyed God and still found himself in the midst of a shaking. Often the noise and shaking shows up to distract you from continuing in what God told us to do. Its primary purpose is to get you to focus on your situation and not your solution – the Word of God. Peter experienced the

154

same thing when walking on the water. Once he stepped out of the boat, in obedience to the Word of God, the wind and waves picked up in their intensity to cause him to take his focus off of Christ – the Word of God.

Understanding No. Two:

The noise and shaking is an attempt to get you to turn around and give up on the change that God has initiated in your life. Often the noisiest and most troublesome times in our life precede the breakthrough that we have been praying for. If you are going through a very noisy and nerve rattling time in your life it may be because you are in the midst of a transition. The noise may be announcing the arrival of a new season in your life.

Understanding No. Three:

This third and final understanding is critical to you experiencing the change that God has begun in your life. *You must continue in your obedience to what God has told you.* The Bible clearly states that because Ezekiel continued to obey God, in the midst of all the confusion, he saw what God had said would happen. Ezekiel's confident confession of God's Word in the midst of a turbulent situation caused everything to fall into their proper place. *"Bone to its bone".* He brought

155

order in the midst of a confusing situation by speaking the Word.

Often, when we're in the midst of a noisy and shaky situation we become so preoccupied with what is wrong that we overlook what God is doing in the midst of the shaking. We can become bitter and unthankful and miss the blessing that God is trying carryout in our lives. *Your shaking may be the beginning of your making.* So if you are in the midst of a shaky situation, continue to do what God has called you to do and don't forget to look around. You just may find that the shaking is setting some things and priorities in their proper place.

Personal Meditations

What is God saying to me through this word?

_____

_____

_____

What adjustments or steps must I take to apply this word in my life?

_____

_____

_____

How has this word affected my approach to, and outlook upon, my life?

_____

_____

_____

Personal Notes & Thoughts:

_____

_____

_____

J.C. MATTHEWS

J.C. MATTHEWS

30

Something Greater

"But I say to you that something greater than the
temple is here."
Matthew 12:6

Someone reading this devotional maybe facing, what appears to be, a seemingly insurmountable situation. They're tired of going in circles, around the same mountain, not knowing any other direction to go in life because something has had them bound. It might be an issue that has persisted over the years or something that has recently manifested itself in their life. Whatever it is, it has caused them to doubt their ability to overcome it, or to live the life God wills for them to live. They've searched for answers but nothing seems sufficient to deal with the mountain that impedes their progress. They've come to the conclusion that they need *something greater* in their life if anything is going to change.

In three separate occasions in scripture, Jesus makes the announcement that *"something greater"* has come. He says that, *"something greater than the temple* (Matt. 12:6)*, Solomon* (Luke 11:3) and *Jonah* (Luke 11:32) *is in our midst.* Something greater and more valuable than the 3 things the Jewish people held in highest esteem; their religion, kings and prophets, was here. Jesus was teaching them not to place their hopes and trust in any limited or earthly resource, but in the One who is *greater* than them all!

Whenever I face a seemingly insurmountable situation, I've discovered that things are not always what they appear to be. The enemy specializes in magnifying our problems, causing us to become preoccupied with them, resulting in fear. Whenever you focus or become preoccupied with anything, it grows in its influence over you. Satan does not want us to come to the revelation that we possess something - - or more precisely *"Someone"* on the inside who is greater than any situation or attack he can launch against us. His objective is to cause us to

160

become fixated on the facts and to take our focus off of our faith in our God.

This is what happened when the children of Israel came to the doorway of their promised land. They magnified their problems and minimize themselves and God who was with them. They saw themselves as mere insects in the face of this giant nation of people. They had forgotten that God, in the not so distant past, brought the mightiest nation on the earth to its knees with insects. Their focus had moved from what God had *promised* to the size of their *problem*. Their problem was not a problem for God! With God on our side, all things are possible - even what appears to be impossible.

What are you facing? What have you been focusing on? Has it been the size of your problem or the strength of your God? Whatever your situation might be, engage it with boldness. You are not alone. Never forget that there is *"Something greater"* in your midst!

J.C. MATTHEWS

Personal Meditations

What is God saying to me through this word?

_____

_____

_____

What adjustments or steps must I take to apply this word in my life?

_____

_____

_____

How has this word affected my approach to, and outlook upon, my life?

_____

_____

_____

Personal Notes & Thoughts:

_____

_____

_____

J.C. MATTHEWS

31

Dealing with Distraction

"Only be strong and very courageous; be careful to do according to all the law which Moses My servant commanded you; do not turn from it to the right or to the left, so that you may have success wherever you go" (Joshua 1:7-8).

In Joshua 1:7-8, God gives us some key principles that we can apply in making the transition from our situation to our destinations. The first thing God warns His people of is the danger of becoming *distracted*. He warns them not to take their focus off of His Word and become distracted by what's going on around them. You will generally encounter distractions when you are getting close to achieving something that will take you to the next level in your life.

Distractions are designed to take your focus off of your future and cause you to become fixated and stuck in your present situation. Some of the most dangerous distractions are those that don't make much noise but creep in while we're at ease. The apparent ease that we enjoy often causes us to forget about the work that still must be done in order for God's promises to manifest in our lives. A season of calm can cause the most diligent of us to become slack in the very thing that got us headed in the right direction. The enemy knows we pray more fervently and are more diligent in our efforts to be delivered, when we're in trouble then when we're at ease. Therefore, he allows a season of "trouble free living", hoping that we will take our focus off of destroying his work, slowing being lulled asleep. Once at ease, we don't discern his activity in our lives and slowly find ourselves struggling with the same things we once overcame. Remember, nothing is truly free unless it comes from God. There is always a cost - even to what appears to be peace.

Often, when we are at ease we allow God to slip into the background of our lives and we slowly drift away from His purpose and plan for our lives. If the truth were told, that is the reason many of us are in the situations we're in now. This is why we must stay focused on where we are going and what we are trying to accomplish.

Distractions also feed of our doubts and fears. When Peter began to walk on the water, he did not sink because he *couldn't finish* what he began to do. He sank because he became distracted and fearful of what was going on around him. As he stepped out and did the impossible, the bible says that the storm around him became more fierce. This is a primary mode of operation of the enemy. If he can't stop you then he will try to distract you. You must be determined to finish what you've begun and be ready to face the certain distractions that will arise.

Your success will be found in your ability to keep your focus on what is ahead of you and not be distracted by what is going on around you. Distractions are not always giants or storm, but can also be found a season of apparent ease. The most dangerous enemy one can face, is an enemy that has not been detected. The Bible promises, *"He will keep him in perfect peace, whose mind is stayed on Him, because he trusts in Him"* (Isaiah 26:3, NKJV).

J.C. MATTHEWS

What is God saying to me through this word?

_____

_____

_____

What adjustments or steps must I take to apply this word in my life?

_____

_____

_____

How has this word affected my approach to, and outlook upon, my life?

_____

_____

_____

Personal Notes & Thoughts:

_____

_____

_____

J.C. MATTHEWS

32

Making Your Way

"This book of the law shall not depart from your mouth, but you shall meditate on it day and night, so that you may be careful to do according to all that is written in it; for then you will make your way prosperous, and then you will have success."
Joshua 1:8

In this text, Joshua and the Nation of Israel are in the midst of making a major life transition. God has brought them out of Egyptian bondage and wandering in an unforgiving wilderness. They are now at the border of a land characterized by abundance. They are making the transition from being slaves in a foreign land, to being owners of their own land. Not only would this be a geographical transition for them, but a mental one as well. God was preparing them to transition from being consumers to producers, borrowers to lenders, to being the head and no longer the tail. God had performed miracle after miracle for them and proven that He was able to provide for them when they couldn't do so for themselves. However, He says to Joshua, in this new season of life, you are going to be responsible for *making "your way prosperous."*

God reveals to Joshua, in this new era of life he's about enter, that He will no longer provide for him the way He did in the past. You will no longer have manna waiting for you in the morning or quail in the evening. In this new place, your provision, protection and success will depend upon your ability to *"do"* My Word. As our situation in life changes, so must our mode of operation. God has a higher and more certain way for us to make our way in life than what we are accustomed too.

In this text, God reveals that the primary means by which we make our way prosperous is by *speaking* His Word. He told Joshua not to allow His Word to *depart from his mouth.* By speaking God's Word we exercise and release the creative power of God's Word into our situation. Speaking God's Word also grows our faith. When we speak God's Word we are also hearing His Word. *"Faith comes by hearing and hearing by the Word of God"* (Romans 10:17).

168

Secondly, God commanded Joshua to continually *"meditate"* on His Word. *Meditation* is the precursor to *manifestation*. Whatever you meditate on will show up in your life. God's Word is the material and substance of all things. God created the world by His Word (Genesis chapter 1, John 1:1-4, Hebrews 11:3, Colossians 1:16). When we meditate on God's Word we are acquiring and assembling what will ultimately manifest in our lives.

Finally, we must be *doers of the word* and not hearers only (James 1:22). God commanded Joshua to *"be careful to do according to all that is written"*. When we have enough confidence and faith in God Word that we are willing to take it from the pages of the Bible and live it, it will accomplish and prosper in the purpose for which it was sent.

This is a new era in your life. Your old way of operating will not work in the new place that God is taking you. We can no longer expect our way to be made by depending on miracles to happen (although God can and will do them if necessary). Our "way" will be made by our *speaking, meditating* and *doing* God's word. If we do this, God has promised, *"then you will make your way prosperous, and then you will have success."*

J.C. MATTHEWS

Personal Meditations

What is God saying to me through this word?

_____

_____

_____

What adjustments or steps must I take to apply this word in my life?

_____

_____

_____

How has this word affected my approach to, and outlook upon, my life?

_____

_____

_____

Personal Notes & Thoughts:

_____

_____

_____

J.C. MATTHEWS

33

The Rewarder

"And without faith it is impossible to please Him, for he who comes to God must believe that He is and that He is a rewarder of those who seek Him" (Hebrews 11:6).

How big is your God? This question might seem ridiculous to many of you but it is a very serious question. God, who is omnipresent (everywhere), omnipotent (all powerful) and omniscience (knows all things) is limited in what He can do in your life by one thing – *your belief and perception of Him.*

That's right, as it pertains to your life, God is confined to the box you place Him in. In the Gospels, Jesus went throughout the countryside performing all kinds of miracle but could not do any in his hometown for those who "knew" Him because of their *unbelief.* The bible says: *"And He could do no miracle ... and He wondered at their unbelief"* (Mark 6:5-6).

When I speak of your belief in God, I am not speaking of a mere acknowledgement of His existence, but a *conviction* of *His preeminence.* If there is anything in your life that you have designated as *impossible* – then your God is too small!

The writer of Hebrews says: *"he who comes to God must believe that He is and that He is a rewarder of those who seek Him"* (Hebrews 11:6).

You must *first, "believe that He is"* **and** secondly, you must believe that *"He is a rewarder of those who seek Him."* God is the ultimate *"Rewarder".* The realization of your breakthrough, deliverance and heart's desire is dependant on both your (1) *belief*, and (2) your expectation of *relief.* Even faith, which is necessary for you to please God, is based upon your *hope* or *expectation. "Faith is the substance of things hoped for...."* (Hebrews 11:1).

Your desire and expectation of God moving in your situation must reach the point that you are willing to thank Him before you see your answer. Remember, believing is only half of the equation. It is in your *expectation* or hope that connects you with your reward.

J.C. MATTHEWS

Personal Meditations

What is God saying to me through this word?

_____
_____
_____

What adjustments or steps must I take to apply this word in my life?

_____
_____
_____

How has this word affected my approach to, and outlook upon, my life?

_____
_____
_____

Personal Notes & Thoughts:

_____
_____
_____

J.C. MATTHEWS

34

Working Twice as Hard

"Take the rod; and you and your brother Aaron
assemble the congregation and speak to the rock
before their eyes, that it may yield its water '.. 'Then
Moses lifted up his hand and struck the rock twice
with his rod; and water came forth abundantly, and
the congregation and their beasts drank. But the
LORD said to Moses and Aaron, " Because you have
not believed Me, to treat Me as holy in the sight of the
sons of Israel, therefore you shall not bring this
assembly into the land which I have given them."
Numbers 20:8-12

When we disobey God we often must work twice as hard to
achieve the same results!

When I began reading this text, something jumped out
and grabbed me. Moses had just performed a miracle by

making water flow from a rock in the middle of the wilderness. The people's needs were met – but something was wrong. *God wasn't pleased.* Moses did the right thing, but he did it the wrong way and hindered what God ultimately wanted to do *through* the miracle. God told Moses to *"speak to the rock before their eyes"* but Moses *"struck the rock twice with his rod".* Many of you maybe saying to yourself, *"What's the difference? The people had their needs met."* The difference is, God was denied the opportunity to teach His people a kingdom principle necessary for them to possess their Promised Land.

The rod Moses struck the rock with was the same rod he used to perform all the signs and wonders with in Egypt and to open the Red Sea. The people had begun to see the *rod* as their source of power and victory instead of *"The Source"* – which is God. God was delivering them into a land where they would no longer be sustained by miracles but by their obedience to God's Word. With the abundance of the Promised Land, it was necessary for them to be able to distinguish between their *"Source"* and *"a resource".* God is our *source.* Everything else is a *resource.* When we confuse the two, we cause what should be a blessing to become a burden.

176

Often, when God directs us to do some thing it doesn't make sense, but it is the best way to achieve the desired result. God has declared,

> *"For My thoughts are not your thoughts, nor are your ways My ways," declares the LORD. "For as the heavens are higher than the earth, so are My ways higher than your ways And My thoughts than your thoughts"* (Isaiah 55:8-9).

God is trying to teach each of us the same thing. When we look to physical things as our source we limit what God can do in our lives. When we trust in His Word, all things are possible. One word from God can change your life. Oftentimes, God *provision* is not a thing but *revelation* - which comes from His Word. Revelation can, in a moment, make plain what you've struggled to figure out for years.

Previously, when Moses caused water to come from a rock, he struck it only once. Because God specifically instructed Moses to speak to the rock, not to strike it, Moses had to work twice a hard. God still performed the miracle. However, it took Moses doing something twice, that God was prepared to do at His Word.

J.C. MATTHEWS

Personal Meditations

What is God saying to me through this word?

_____

_____

_____

What adjustments or steps must I take to apply this word in my life?

_____

_____

_____

How has this word affected my approach to, and outlook upon, my life?

_____

_____

_____

Personal Notes & Thoughts:

_____

_____

_____

J.C. MATTHEWS

35

Faith in the Between Times

"Martha then said to Jesus, "Lord, if You had been here, my brother would not have died. "Even now I know that whatever You ask of God, God will give You." Jesus said to her, "Your brother will rise again." Martha said to Him, "I know that he will rise again in the resurrection on the last day." Jesus said to her, "I am the resurrection and the life; he who believes in Me will live even if he dies, and everyone who lives and believes in Me will never die. Do you believe this?" She said to Him, "Yes, Lord; I have believed that You are the Christ, the Son of God, even He who comes into the world" (John 11:21-27).

Martha was a witness of what Jesus *had done* in the lives of others. She expressed her faith concerning the *future*

J.C. MATTHEWS

and our resurrection from the dead. However, she struggled to maintain her faith concerning her own dead situation that she was dealing with right now. She needed faith for the *"in-between times"* of life.

Martha's struggle is also our struggle. Like Martha, some of us have called upon God for help and things seem to have only grown worse. How do we maintain our faith in the face of facts that seem insurmountable? Many of us have no problem believing that God delivered the three Hebrew boys from their fiery furnace or that He provided for a multitude with only two fish and five loaves of bread. However, when it comes down to our own deliverance and Him meeting our own needs we are not so sure. The "in between times" in our lives are the time between our having heard and believed the Word of God and it manifesting in our lives.

Faith by its very definition is for the *"in between times"* of life. It is both present tense and futuristic in nature. Hebrews 11:1 declares, ***"Now faith is...."*** Faith is for our *right now*! We develop *"in between time faith"* by *deciding right now* that we believe God and His Word more than our circumstances. While Martha stood in front of her dead brother's tomb, Jesus asked her if she believed that He in-fact was life. When she answered *"Yes"*, she released faith into her situation, which possessed

180

the substance of what she hoped for (resurrection), and the evidence of what she had not seen - *"yet"*. It is our exercise of faith in the midst of our situation that releases the power of God. The most powerful kind of faith is faith that is exercised *"in the between times"*.

God may be using that *impossibility* in your life as an *opportunity* for you to exercise your faith during the *"in between time"*. This is when real faith is proven. Faith comes by hearing, and hearing by the word of God (Romans 10:17). Faith begins when you hear the word and must be maintained until you see its manifestation. Remember, that every miracle in the Bible had its beginning in midst of someone's impossibility. It was their faith during the *"in between time"* that caused them to see what they had previously only heard of!

J.C. MATTHEWS

Personal Meditations

What is God saying to me through this word?

_____

_____

_____

What adjustments or steps must I take to apply this word in
my life?

_____

_____

_____

How has this word affected my approach to, and outlook upon,
my life?

_____

_____

_____

Personal Notes & Thoughts:

_____

_____

_____

J.C. MATTHEWS

36

Stopping the Cycle of Self Destruction

"I said to them, "We according to our ability have redeemed our Jewish brothers who were sold to the nations; now would you even sell your brothers that they may be sold to us?" Then they were silent and could not find a word to say" (Nehemiah 5:8, NASB).

In this text, Nehemiah addresses a very serious issue that hindered his people in their efforts to restore what was broken and lost in their lives. If you read chapters 1 through 4 of the book of Nehemiah and then read Chapter 5, it seems out of place. Chapters 1 through 4 tell us how the work began and the progress they were making. We are also introduced to their enemies who conspired together to stop the work the people have begun. Chapter 4 ends with Nehemiah's plan to continue the work in the face of possible attack by their enemies. However, in Chapter 5, we discover a problem much greater than an invading army. We discover that the real enemy is not an external one, but an internal one.

As the days passed and the work continued, I believe Nehemiah began to notice a drop in the progress they were making. It was as if they had reached a certain point in the restoration process and could go no further. They had not been attacked by an enemy but seemed defeated. The people were saying amongst themselves:

"The strength of the burden bearers is failing, yet there is much rubbish; and we ourselves are unable to rebuild the wall" *(Nehemiah. 4:10).*

They were saying they *could not do* something they were *already doing* – rebuilding the wall. As a result, Nehemiah began to search for a cause and discovered that there indeed was an enemy in the camp - *themselves!*

The people were not only speaking against the work they were trying to finish but were enslaving one another as well. They had been captive for so long, under Babylonian and Persian rule, *captivity* became their *mentality.* Nehemiah, in Chapter

5:8 tells the people, "We worked hard for our freedom, but now you're repeating the same cycle we've been delivered from" (paraphrased). They were repeating a negative learned behavior. They tore down with their own hands the very thing they were trying to build – their identity. The very people necessary to rebuild the wall they were enslaving, thereby hindering the restoration process. They were repeating a cycle of *self-destruction.*

Oftentimes, people subconsciously hinder what God is doing in their life by saying and doing things that are contrary to what they are trying to achieve. They may lash out at people that try to help them because they may be afraid of change or the unfamiliar.

Self-destruction is the enemy's weapon of *mass destruction!* More hopes and dreams have been killed by *"friendly fire"* than *"enemy fire".* Many Believers consciously and unconsciously participate in cycles of self-destructive behavior. They destroy the very things they are trying to build with their actions and words. Like the wall, they've lived with brokenness for so long that brokenness has become commonplace - even expected.

If you continue to experience the same disappointments and failures in life, even when the circumstances are favorable, you may be consciously or unconsciously stuck in a cycle of self-destruction. Breaking the cycle of *"self-destruction"* starts with your building your *"self perception"*.

The enemy wants you to develop a mentality of failure so that you forfeit the opportunities and blessing that God places in your life. When the people examined themselves instead of focusing on others, the Bible records in the first verse of the next chapter (Chapter 6) that, they finally *"finished the wall"*. Their *restoration* was facilitated by the *revelation* that *my real enemy* is really *"in me!"*

J.C. MATTHEWS

Personal Meditations

What is God saying to me through this word?

_____
_____
_____

What adjustments or steps must I take to apply this word in
my life?

_____
_____
_____

How has this word affected my approach to, and outlook upon,
my life?

_____
_____
_____

Personal Notes & Thoughts:

_____
_____
_____

J.C. MATTHEWS

J.C. MATTHEWS

37

He is "Still" Worthy

*"Then Job arose and tore his robe and shaved his
head, and he fell to the ground and worshiped."*
Job 1:20, NASB

Most American, and those from around the world, find themselves in the midst of a transition in their lives. People are losing their homes, personal property, jobs and even loved ones. Many have been thrust into the midst of a turbulent transition without an adequate explanation. They did not thing wrong to deserve the storm, but none the less find themselves in the midst of a raging one. One moment they were surrounded by family and friends and the next they find themselves all alone. They're asking questions that no one seems to have answers for. Many of them are asking: How am I going to make it? Where do I go from here? How could this happen to me? Why did it happen?

Your storm may have manifested itself in the form of a divorce, bankruptcy, loss of a job, home, or the betrayal by a loved one or some other situation that left you exhausted and in a position of vulnerability. You can't change what has happened, but you do control your response too what has happened. How you respond to your situation will determine your outcome.

I am going to suggest something that may sound strange to the contemporary ear, but its truth resounds throughout eternity. I want to suggest that: *"The proper response in the aftermath of your situation, is "worship!"* That's right, I said worship, not worry! Considering all that has happened, the way through and above it all is to worship God. In the midst of all of the pain, bitterness, loss and frustration we must find a way to focus on His perfection and power as our source and strength.

I won't pretend to understand what you have been through, but I would like to call upon someone who can look you in the eye and proclaim: "No matter what you're going through, the pathway to your restoration is to worship God!" This someone's
190

name is "Job". Like some of you, Job lost everything he had, at no fault of his own. Those closest to him - including his wife, rejected him. To make matters worse, the devil himself (not some lower ranking demon) personally set out to destroy him. In light of all of this the Bible says Job: *"arose and ... worshipped"* (Job 1:20).

We find a similar response by King David after his first child by Bathsheba died. The Bible says: *"David arose from the ground ... and he came into the house of the LORD and worshiped"* (2 Samuel 12:20).

When you worship God you create an atmosphere and an avenue by which He can begin the restoration process. Both David and Job were completely restored after their decision to proclaim God's worthiness in the midst of their situation. God can turn your situation around for the better just as quickly as it changed for the worse. Your situation may change, but God never changes. He was, He is and will always be worthy of our praise! Therefore, worship Him! Worship Him!! Worship Him!!! For HE is still - Worthy!!!!

J.C. MATTHEWS

What is God saying to me through this word?

_____

_____

_____

What adjustments or steps must I take to apply this word in my life?

_____

_____

_____

How has this word affected my approach to, and outlook upon, my life?

_____

_____

_____

Personal Notes & Thoughts:

_____

_____

_____

J.C. MATTHEWS

38

The Fine Line Between Faith and Foolishness

"And He said to them, "When I sent you out without money belt and bag and sandals, you did not lack anything, did you?" They said, "No, nothing." And He said to them, "But now, whoever has a money belt is to take it along, likewise also a bag, and whoever has no sword is to sell his coat and buy one. "
Luke 22:34-36

It would be foolishness for you to obey someone who told you to drive to the other side of the country and not take any clothing, food, money or protection for the trip. This is basically what Jesus instructed His disciples to do. In our text,

J.C. MATTHEWS

Jesus had previously told His disciples to go and spread the gospel without taking the usual precautions prudent men and women traveling for an extended period of time, in uncertain territory would take. However, Jesus later tells them that when they go out this time, to take with them the very same things He initially told them to leave behind. What changed? In the first instance Jesus was trying to teach them about faith. What would the result be if they took the same journey, after Jesus told them to they now needed to take the necessary provision, without taking the things needed? The results would be tragic. As a matter of fact, it wouldn't be *faith* at all - it would be *foolishness*. There is a fine line between faith and foolishness.

One of the greatest struggles for Believers is trying to discern when God is calling them to attempt something naturally impossible but is required for them to grow in their relationship and faith walk with Him. Do I use common sense or do I, "*walk by faith and not by sight*" (2Cor. 5:7). Some of greatest victories witnessed in the Bible were the result of individuals walking by faith and not sight. In 1 Kings 17:8-17, Elijah told a widow in the midst of a famine, who was preparing a small cake for herself and her son to eat and die, to give him the last of what she had. In Judges 7:1-8, God told Gideon to prune down his army from over 100,000 fighting

194

men to only 300 – and the list goes on. In all of these situations, these individuals exercised their faith and did what didn't make sense.

Many of you are likewise confronted with situations that seem insurmountable and wonder if God is calling you to move forward in faith, regardless of how things appear, or to use caution and common sense in dealing with the situation. There is no question, that as we grow in our faith, that God will require us to move forward in situations that seem dim but are actually the doorway to the deliverance we seek. God is not a God of confusion and has not left us without direction.

There are 3 characteristics of a faith situation that are unique and distinctive from others we might face. Knowing these characteristics will enable us to confidently move forward in faith and experience the victory God has for us. First, *We must have a biblical foundation for doing the endeavor.* In other words, the action must be the result of the Word God. God never contradicts His revealed Word. Second, *There is a kingdom purpose involved.* The question to ask is, *"Will God's Kingdom be advanced or glorified by its accomplishment?"* God is not obliged to advance our agendas, but He is obliged to advance His Kingdom. Third, *it must be done "in season".* The Bible declares that there is a time and season for everything

J.C. MATTHEWS

under the sun. Often when God calls for us to do something by faith, it calls for our prompt obedience. In one season of the disciples walk with Jesus told them not to take money, extra clothing or a sword for their travels. However, after Jesus finished teaching them this lesson, they no longer can expect the same results they experienced previously, if they were to try the same thing again. Its timing had passed.

Their actions would not be supported by *the Word*, nor would it advance a Kingdom purpose. By keeping this in mind we can avoid the frustration of believing God for something He has not promised. Remember, there is a fine line between what is of faith and what is foolish!

Personal Meditations

What is God saying to me through this word?

_____

_____

_____

What adjustments or steps must I take to apply this word in
my life?

_____

_____

_____

How has this word affected my approach to, and outlook upon,
my life?

_____

_____

_____

Personal Notes & Thoughts:

_____

_____

_____

J.C. MATTHEWS

J.C. MATTHEWS

39

Healed and Whole

"And Jesus said, Somebody hath touched me: for I perceive that virtue is gone out of me. And when the woman saw that she was not hid, she came trembling, and falling down before him, she declared unto him before all the people for what cause she had touched him, and how she was healed immediately. And he said unto her, Daughter, be of good comfort: thy faith hath made thee whole; go in peace" (Luke 8:45-48, KJV).

Too often, the extremity of our situation causes us to settle for something that may be *better* than what we're dealing with, but it is definitely not the *best* God has planned for us. These short sighted circumstantial decisions short change us from experiencing the wholeness God desires for our lives.

In our text, we find a woman who the Bible describes as having *"an"* issue of blood. However, experience testifies, that rarely are the issues of life solitary ones. Some issues may be more pronounced than others, but that does not make them any less problematic. The Bible expressly states, that this woman suffered physically from hemorrhage, as well as, financial ruin due to her seeking a cure for her condition. We can safely infer that she also suffered mentally and socially due to her being legally prohibited from being around others, and her worsening condition. Physical healing was only one of the many issues this woman faced day to day. However, when her physical condition was bettered by Jesus, she walked away satisfied. I believe Jesus discerned in this women's touch that: (1) there were other issues in this woman's life, and (2) she possessed the potential for her to receive much more than physical healing. She had powerful faith. Faith powerful enough to withdrawal from healing that wasn't found anywhere else in the world. However, her expectations were too low and shortsighted. Jesus wasn't going to allow her to settle for anything less than His best. God not only wanted her healed, He wanted her made *whole!*

After Jesus called her forward, He declared that she was not only *healed*, but that her *faith* had made her *whole!* Her ability

200

to believe by faith, that God could do what everyone else could not do, opened the door for God to not only deal with her health, but to minister to the other issue in her life. Healing is only a component of wholeness - but it is not the sum total of it. Just like money is only a component of prosperity, it is not the sum total of prosperity. I believe, not only was she was restored in her health, but her mind, spirit and relationships.

What is it you are expecting God to do in your life? Are you only seeking relief from a symptom or are you seeking deliverance from the symptoms source? This woman only sought healing. Healing would have been all she received if Jesus had not let her know that He was willing and able to do much more. Our *expectation* in life defines and determines the level of *manifestation* in our lives. God is able to do *"exceedingly, abundantly, above all you can ask or think ..."* (Eph. 3:20). The same faith it took for the woman to be healed of her hemorrhage, was the same faith God used to declare her whole! Does this sound like your life? If not, you may have experienced *better* in your life, but have yet to taste God's best! *He not only wants you healed – He wants you whole!*

J.C. MATTHEWS

Personal Meditations

What is God saying to me through this word?

_____

_____

_____

What adjustments or steps must I take to apply this word in my life?

_____

_____

_____

How has this word affected my approach to, and outlook upon, my life?

_____

_____

_____

Personal Notes & Thoughts:

_____

_____

_____

J.C. MATTHEWS

40

Your Answer Is At The Door

"So Peter was kept in prison, but the church was earnestly praying to God for him' ... 'Suddenly an angel of the Lord appeared and a light shone in the cell. He struck Peter on the side and woke him up. "Quick, get up!" he said, and the chains fell off Peter's wrists'. ... 'When this had dawned on him, he went to the house of Mary the mother of John, also called Mark, where many people had gathered and were praying. Peter knocked at the outer entrance, and a servant girl named Rhoda came to answer the door. When she recognized Peter's voice, she was so overjoyed she ran back without opening it and exclaimed, "Peter is at the door!" "You're out of your mind," they told her. When she kept insisting that it was so, they said, "It must be his angel." But Peter kept on knocking, and when they opened the door and saw him, they were astonished.
(Acts 12:5,7,12-16, NIV)

J.C. MATTHEWS

One morning during my prayer and devotion time, I ran across a scripture that stopped me in my tracks. There was something in the text that God wanted me to see. So I backed up and reread the text again. Then it hit me! These believers, who were praying earnestly, weren't expecting their prayers to be answered. I said to myself: *"How can this be? How can we prayer "earnestly" for something and not believe our answer when it arrives?"* God revealed to me that this happens all the time. He sends answers to our prayers and they are returned to Him stamped *"Unclaimed."*

Why is this? How can we take the time to pray and not expect our answer or recognize it when it comes knocking? I believe there are three main reasons why this happens.

First, is a *"lack of expectation"* **due to** *"past experiences"*. In looking at the context of this scripture, these individuals had experienced fellow believers being killed, even after they prayed for their release. They had endured the stoning of Stephen, the slaying of James and now their leader Peter was schedule to be next. Those who were in the house praying, told the young girl who reported that their prayers had been answered, that she was *"out of her mind"*. However, we must remember that our past experiences or failures do not determine or dictate God's present or future course of action.
204

We must expect God to answer our prayers and be on the look out for its manifestation in our lives, regardless of what happened yesterday. The Bible says that *he who comes to God must believe that He is and that He is a rewarder of those who diligently seek Him* (Hebrews 11:6).

Secondly, prayer in the lives of many believers, has become simply a *"religious activity or responsibility"* **instead of it being the heaven moving gift of God.** When we lose sight of the fact that we are calling upon an all knowing, all powerful, Creator God of the universe, who also happens to be *"our Father"*, we can become overwhelmed by the severity of our situation. We must understand that we are not calling upon another human being or some distant disinterested deity - but our Father who has no limitations. If I can find it in His Word, and agree with what He has said, the facts of my situation will have to line up with the truth of His word. Facts change everyday, but the truth never changes. Because I've decided to believe the truth above the fluctuating facts, I have a legitimate expectation of manifestation (answered pray) in my life. Prayer is more than a religious activity or a believer's responsibility, but a relationship with our Father!

Thirdly, "God's ways are not our ways". I truly believe, that part of the difficulty those gathered in prayer had in receiving

J.C. MATTHEWS

their answer, was that it seemed *"too easy"*. They prayed and God answered their prayer. It was that simple! Believe it or not, this happens more often than you think. I've discovered that many of us overlook our answers because we *"feel"* that we haven't toiled, labored or suffered enough to have earned an answer from God. Remember, you are a "son", not a slave! You don't *earn* blessings - you *receive* them! Jesus said, in Matthew 7:11, *"If you, then, though you are evil, know how to give good gifts to your children, how much more will your Father in heaven give good gifts to those who ask him!"*

Therefore, what have you been praying to God about? Did you know that God is your Father and He wants to bless you? Do you expect your prayer to be answered? If not, you need to take a good look around, because the answer to your prayer may have already arrived, and waiting on you to claim it!

J.C. MATTHEWS

Personal Meditations

What is God saying to me through this word?

_____

_____

_____

What adjustments or steps must I take to apply this word in my life?

_____

_____

_____

How has this word affected my approach to, and outlook upon, my life?

_____

_____

_____

Personal Notes & Thoughts:

_____

_____

_____

J.C. MATTHEWS

J.C. MATTHEWS

Additional Copies of this book and other titles
from Blessed Books Publishing can be obtained
by faxing a request to 972-767-3056 or by
sending your request to:

Blessed Books Publishing
P.O. Box 360102
Irving, Texas 75063

BLESSED BOOKS
PUBLISHING CO.

J.C. MATTHEWS

J.C. MATTHEWS

About the Author

Dr. J.C. Matthews is a noted author, teacher, speaker and the visionary founding Pastor of Dunamis Life Ministries of Dallas, Texas. Dr. Matthews is known for his love of God's Word, wisdom and gift for practically applying scripture to everyday life. He has authored several books and is a noted devotional writer for various Christian media outlets.

Dr. Matthews possesses a B.A. in Political Science, as well as a Juris Doctorate (J.D.) degree. While in law school J.C. was twice recognized for his outstanding study of law by his induction into the "Who's Who Among American Law Students". He has also been honored as an Urban All-American by the General Assembly of the Ohio State Senate.

Dr. Matthews lives in the Dallas / Ft. Worth Texas area with his wife Gena and four children.

To contact or schedule Pastor Matthews please do so by visiting www.jcmatthewsminitries.com.

J.C. MATTHEWS

J.C. MATTHEWS

Here are more titles by J.C. Matthews.

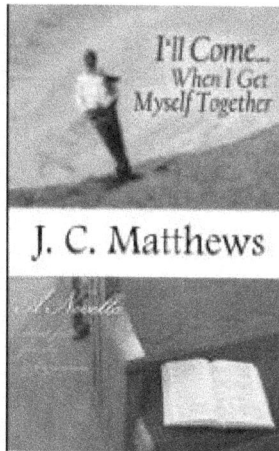

For more information concerning other resources offered by J.C. Matthews, please visit: www.jcmatthewsministries.com

J.C. MATTHEWS

214

J.C. MATTHEWS

Also Available

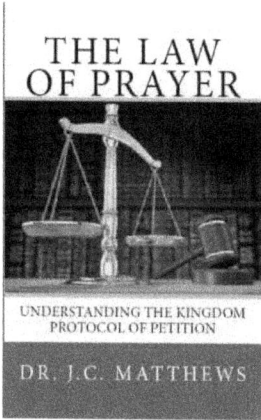

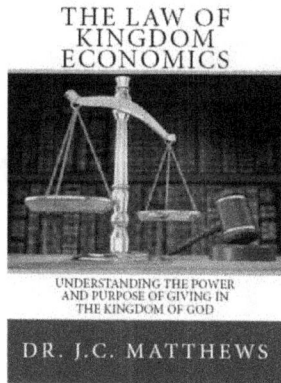

THE LAW OF PRAYER

UNDERSTANDING THE KINGDOM
PROTOCOL OF PETITION

DR. J.C. MATTHEWS

THE KINGDOM'S LABOR LAWS

REDISCOVERING THE KEYS TO
EXPERIENCING A FRUITFUL
AND FULFILLING LIFE

DR. J.C. MATTHEWS

THE LAW OF KINGDOM ECONOMICS

UNDERSTANDING THE POWER
AND PURPOSE OF GIVING IN
THE KINGDOM OF GOD

DR. J.C. MATTHEWS

Check out www.blessedbookspublishing.com for more titles from this series for dates of release and availability.

J.C. MATTHEWS

J.C. MATTHEWS